The Yorkshire Witch

The Yorkshire Witch

The Life and Trial of Mary Bateman

Summer Strevens

First published in Great Britain in 2017 by
Pen & Sword History
an imprint of
Pen & Sword Books Ltd
47 Church Street
Barnsley
South Yorkshire
S70 2AS

ISBN 978 1 47386 387 3

A CIP catalogue record for this book is available from the British Library

Typeset in Ehrhardt by
Mac Style Ltd, Bridlington, East Yorkshire
Printed and bound in the UK by CPI Group (UK) Ltd,
Croydon, CRO 4YY

Pen & Sword Books Ltd incorporates the imprints of Pen & Sword Archaeology, Atlas, Aviation, Battleground, Discovery, Family History, History, Maritime, Military, Naval, Politics, Railways, Select, Transport, True Crime, and Fiction, Frontline Books, Leo Cooper, Praetorian Press, Seaforth Publishing and Wharncliffe.

For a complete list of Pen & Sword titles please contact
PEN & SWORD BOOKS LIMITED
47 Church Street, Barnsley, South Yorkshire, S70 2AS, England
E-mail: enquiries@pen-and-sword.co.uk
Website: www.pen-and-sword.co.uk

Contents

Acknowledgements vi
Introduction ix

Chapter 1 'A knavish and vicious disposition' 1

Chapter 2 Mrs Moore's Screws 18

Chapter 3 From The Hand Of Miss Blythe 33

Chapter 4 'Crist is coming' 42

Chapter 5 A Long Distance Dupe 54

Chapter 6 'My dear Friend…' 67

Chapter 7 The End of a Crooked Road 80

Chapter 8 The Gates Of Mercy Are Closed 90

Chapter 9 'Quick' with Child? 104

Chapter 10 'Damn her name to everlasting fame' 120

Bibliography and Sources 137
Index 139

Acknowledgements

At the risk of opening these acknowledgements after the fashion of a scant bibliography, I would firstly like to express my particular indebtedness to the anonymous author (whom I have tentatively identified in the last chapter of this book) who first undertook to set down the only contemporary account of Mary Bateman's life and exploits, shortly after her execution, now over two hundred years ago. Understandably, I have drawn heavily from the volubly titled *The Extraordinary life and character of Mary Bateman The Yorkshire Witch traced from the earliest thefts of her infancy through a most awful course of crimes and murders till her execution at the castle of York, on the 20th March, 1809* – though this must be considered as something of a sensationalised and indeed unsubstantiated account in parts. Necessarily circumnavigating the moralising tone so typical of the age, the book nevertheless proved an invaluable source, as did William Knipe's *Criminal Chronology of York Castle*, the full title of which is as tumescent as the former publication, and though censorious in damningly equivalent measure, nonetheless provided many valuable insights in the research of this book.

In addition, though largely borrowing from *The Extraordinary Life*, the second volume of *The Criminal Recorder: or, Biographical sketches of Notorious Public Characters*, again anonymously written in 1815 by a 'Student of the Inner Temple' provided some further pertinent particulars, as did the colourful, albeit brief, account of Mary's life and crimes as reported by *The Newgate Calendar*, (the hugely popular monthly bulletin, yet a supposedly moralising publication that gave vivid accounts of notorious criminals in the eighteenth and nineteenth centuries, and which did not disappoint in the report of Mary's case, the culmination of the opening line running thus, that: 'she richly deserved that fate which eventually befell her'.

My acknowledgments to the living however must include my effusive thanks to Lauren Ryall-Stockton and Catherine Robins, Curator and Assistant Curator respectively of the Thackray Medical Museum, Leeds, who were unreserved in their assistance with regards to my enquiries concerning one of the Thackray's most iconic (and possibly most controversial) exhibits, namely the display of Mary Bateman's partial skeleton. I am also deeply indebted to Dr Dave Roberts, Senior Lecturer in Anatomy, University of Leeds School of Medicine, who was kind enough to indulge my scant anatomical knowledge, in addition to clarifying for me the University's policy concerning the display and indeed future destiny of Mary Bateman's remains, still the property of the University. Grateful thanks are also due to Fiona Munroe Blyth, former director of the United Kingdom Association for Transactional Analysis, who assisted in providing an invaluable insight into theories of modern psychology.

With regards to archival documentary research, further thanks are due for the research support kindly provided by Rose Gibson, Central Library Manager of Leeds Library, and the Leeds Library Information Service who manage the 'Leodis' online archive which as well as containing over 59,000 images of Leeds, old and new, is a wonderful repository of historical information pertinent to the city's past. I would also like to thank Robert Wake, Collections Facilitator for York Museums Trust, for providing access to and permission for use of material held in the York Castle Museum archives, as well as Fiona Marshall and Malcolm Mathieson, Archivists for the West

Yorkshire Archive Service. I should also like to extend my gratitude to Simon Craddock, Library Assistant with the Yorkshire Archaeological Society and to George P Landow, Founder and Editor-in-chief of *The Victorian Web*, an invaluable source for historical images of Leeds. Mention must also be made of Andrew Currie, Deputy Director of Press and Public Relations for Bonhams of London in securing the rare image of one of Joanna Southcott's 'seals'. I would also like to thank the Reverend Susanne Jukes, Vicar of St Columba, Topcliffe, for her assistance in tracking down Mary Bateman's baptismal record, now in the care of the North Yorkshire County Records Office, and to Jan Reed for her unstinting efforts in obtaining a copy of the same.

Special commendation is also due to my publishers, and in particular I also wish to acknowledge the support, advice and infinite forbearance of my editor, Carol Trow. Finally, I am indebted to my partner, Jack Gritton, without whose enduring patience and support in the face of my woeful IT abilities I would have been lost.

To all those mentioned above, and everyone else who has given of their time, guided and shared in their professional knowledge and insights, Thank You.

Summer Strevens
2017

Introduction

On the morning of 20 March 1809, a Monday, the usual day designated for the execution of murderers, the woman who had earned herself the title of 'The Yorkshire Witch' was executed upon York's New Drop gallows, hanged before a crowd variously estimated at between five and twenty thousand people. Among the multitude who came to see Mary Bateman die were some who had travelled all the way from her home town of Leeds, many of them on foot, and doubtless many of them the victims of her hoaxes and extortions.

I first came across Mary while researching another book on the criminal history of York. Though not a witch in the traditional sense, Mary Bateman was what we would term today a consummate con-artist – a charlatan of the first order, a compulsive liar, confidence trickster, thief and fraudster, who, through her 'artifice and deleterious skill', deceived many victims by instilling in them the belief that she had supernatural powers. According to contemporary accounts, Mary was charismatic and ostensibly charming and above all extremely adept at identifying the psychological weaknesses of the gullible. Easily gaining the simple trust placed in the her by the desperate and poor who populated the growing industrial metropolis of Leeds at the turn of the nineteenth century, she was a supreme exponent of the art of exploiting their fears and ancient folk memory of witchcraft to rob them of all their worldly goods. Mary however, did much more than cause misery and penury, adding murder to the list of her diabolical deeds.

Along with the theft of money and goods, Mary increasingly turned to fortune-telling as her main source of income – it was said that through exposure to gypsies in her early life, she had learnt many of their arts – and embellished her prophesies with the wisdom she sought from a Mrs Moore whom Mary always consulted on behalf of her clients. Incidentally, the lady was pure invention on Mary's part, but this didn't stop her from taking payment on Mrs Moore's behalf. While the mystical and mythical Mrs Moore, whose supernatural powers apparently stemmed from her being the seventh child of a seventh child, proved a profitable invention, Mary was also to employ the services of the equally fictitious Miss Blythe. Adept at seeing into the future and an exponent in the removal of evil spells and the provision of magical cures, of course, through the agency of Mary, Miss Blythe charged exorbitantly for her expertise.

While Mary Bateman was tried and convicted on a single murder charge, we can say with a measure of certainty that she killed at least three others, and in all probability was responsible for many more deaths that escaped detection. The labelling of Mary Bateman as a serial killer, the term and concept first coined by German criminologist Ernst Gennat in 1930, certainly fits with the definition – someone who murders more than three victims, one at a time in a relatively short interval. Gennat was Director of the Berlin Criminal Police in the early Nazi years. His work on notorious murderers Fritz Haarmann and Peter Kurten led to the *serienmorder* phrase, although both men's crimes had a sexual element totally missing from Mary's. Research has shown that the predominant impetus for serial killers is based on psychological gratification. Motives including thrill, attention seeking and financial gain, the latter of which certainly drove Mary. She resorted to theft and fraud on an impressive scale, later escalating to the elimination of her victims, a necessary and expedient measure against their discovery and exposure of the ruthless pact into which they had entered with the Yorkshire Witch. The hypothesis that Mary suffered from a psychological condition which drove her criminal behaviour is discussed in the last chapter of this book.

Murder aside, Mary's most audacious and far reaching deception centred on a phenomenon that became known as 'The Prophet Hen of Leeds', a doomsday scam engineered to play on the fears of those persuaded to believe that the Second Coming of Jesus Christ was imminent. While there have been countless examples of people who have proclaimed that the return of Jesus Christ is at hand (most recently, in October 2014 the image of Christ appearing on a slice of wholemeal toast in Manchester was hailed as such a sign), possibly there has never been a stranger messenger than the chicken that laid eggs on which the phrase 'Crist is coming' was indelibly written. As news of this miracle spread, many people became convinced that the End Days were looming – and paid hard cash to see Mary's miracle hen. Until, that is, a curious local doctor discovered that Mary herself was responsible for literally 'hatching a hoax', but not before she had managed to turn a healthy profit. The reputation of Joanna Southcott, whose flourishing following by those spiritually devoted to her ideals was also adversely affected by Mary's exploitative association with the self-proclaimed prophetess.

It is a testament to Mary's contemporary notoriety that the book published in 1811, two years after her execution, and detailing her life and crimes ran to a twelfth edition. As the inordinately lengthy title suggests *The Extraordinary Life and Character of Mary Bateman, the Yorkshire Witch; Traced from the Earliest thefts of Her Infancy, Through a Most Awful Course of Crimes and Murders, Till Her Execution at the New Drop, Near the Castle of York, on Monday the Twentieth Of March, 1809*, the book detailed how her 'knavish and vicious disposition' began to show at the tender age of five, and developed into the many frauds, deceptions and ultimately murder which marked her later life as that of a career criminal. Yet, through remarkable luck and cunning, Mary managed to evade the grasp of the authorities for over twenty years, during which time she ruined many lives, as well as taking them, lacing her charms and cures with arsenic.

Amongst those who fell victim to Mary's malign ministrations were the Misses Kitchin, two Quaker sisters who kept a draper's shop in Leeds and who fell for Mary's ingratiating ways. In the space of ten days, both sisters died mysteriously, along with their mother, after taking medicines prescribed by Mary, all three ending up in a shared grave. And as a practising abortionist, Mary must invariably have been responsible for any number of unrecorded fatalities of those young women who sought her assistance in terminating an unwanted pregnancy. However, it was for the murder of Rebecca Perigo for which Mary was tried, convicted and hanged. At the time of her arrest, Mary was poised to poison again, and may very well have succeeded had it not been for the timely account in a Leeds newspaper, exposing and alerting her next potential victims to the danger they were in.

While Mary Bateman's status as a 'witch' gave cause to sensationalise her death, over two hundred years after her execution, the macabre display of her (partial) skeleton still proved a great draw for visitors to the Thackray Medical Museum in Leeds. The bones were on long-term loan from Leeds University Anatomy Department where Mary's body was dissected. Some would say that this barbaric treatment of her corpse was an apt punishment for her crimes. Described by the Museum as one of their iconic exhibits, the continuous display of Mary's skeleton since the Thackray first opened in 1997 until the recent decision to remove her remains in July 2015 was, and still is, a bone of contention – literally you might say – with regards to the ethical and moral position of her remains still being denied Christian burial.

Despite the notoriety attached to the name of the Yorkshire Witch and the continuing controversy surrounding her post-mortem fate,

Mary Bateman remains something of an ethereal character. After two centuries, it is difficult to be accurate about her motivation. In some ways she is a shadow, blurred still further by the passage of time. The fact that Mary's crimes are catalogued in various sensational accounts of infamous villainesses proves the public's fascination, still as potent today as in her own time. It is all the more extraordinary then that this is the first biography exclusively dedicated to Mary Bateman since the aforementioned anonymously written and heavily moralising account which appeared in print two years after her execution on York's gallows.

Certainly, in the words of *The Extraordinary Life,* her character was evil enough to 'Damn her name to everlasting fame'. This book in no way seeks to vindicate the actions of a convicted murderess, but we must weigh the moralising strictures and harsh sentiment that were the hallmarks of her time, and look at her upbringing, background and the social milieu in which she existed. In turn we must examine the effects of a burgeoning industrial revolution on her and everyone else's environment. That way a more complete picture of Mary will emerge, engendering an appreciation that people in the past were not just 'good' or 'bad', but motivated by personal and societal complexities and conflicts, just as we are today.

Author's note: In view of the overly lengthy title of the '*The Extraordinary Life and Character of Mary Bateman, the Yorkshire Witch; Traced from the Earliest thefts of Her Infancy, Through a Most Awful Course of Crimes and Murders, Till Her Execution at the New Drop, Near the Castle of York, on Monday the Twentieth Of March, 1809*', henceforth where referred to throughout the text, the title of this publication will be abbreviated to *The Extraordinary Life*.

Summer Strevens
2017

Chapter 1

'A knavish and vicious disposition'

When Mary Bateman was born, she was of so little importance that the date of her birth went unrecorded. When it came to her final moments on the gallows however, thousands of spectators witnessed her execution upon York's 'New Drop' on the morning of Monday 20 March 1809, some of whom, packed shoulder to shoulder in the crowd, were convinced to the very end that the Yorkshire Witch would save herself from death at the last moment by employing her supernatural powers to vanish into thin air as the noose tightened. Needless to say, she didn't.

Mary was forty-one at the time of her execution, and while her exact birth date is not known, the parish records of St Columba, Topcliffe, in the North Riding of Yorkshire, show her as being baptised on 15 January 1768. English parish registers as a general rule recorded baptisms rather than births, so we can assume that she was born late in 1767 or early 1768, as the average age at baptism increased from one week old in the middle of the seventeenth century to one month by the middle of the nineteenth century. The church itself, with its fourteenth century interior fittings, was extensively rebuilt in the 1880s. Born Mary Harker in Asenby, a town in the parish of Topcliffe on the south bank of the River Swale, a few miles south of the larger market town of Thirsk, she was the third of six children born to Benjamin Harker and his wife Ann, née Dunning. Benjamin and Ann had married at Brompton by Northallerton on 10 July 1754, before moving to Asenby, a little less than fifteen miles away, to take up small scale farming.

Asenby today remains a small village with less than 300 inhabitants, with the majority of the surrounding land still given over to farming. However, when the Harkers took up residence, every cottage and farmstead would have been entirely familiar and every face known; any stranger passing through would have caused a stir, the odd pedlar, or a sailor making his way home from sea across country exciting comment.

The decade of Mary's birth was a momentous one. In London, the new king, George III, came under increasing attack from the satirist John Wilkes at the same time that trouble was brewing in the thirteen British colonies in America. At home, the economic and social upheaval we now call the Industrial Revolution was beginning to gain momentum of its own. The Harkers were the last generation to live off the land – their children were city dwellers.

The couple's first child and Mary's eldest sister, Jane, was born at Brompton and baptised there in the parish church of St Thomas, where her parents had been married, on 7 August 1755. The church we see today is much altered from the one they knew. It was still a chapel of ease to All Saints' Northallerton at the time but was heavily rebuilt in 1867. Her subsequent siblings were all born at Asenby: Ann, named for her mother was baptised 28 April 1765; then after the birth of Mary came Elizabeth, baptised on 17 September 1770; Benjamin, named for his father, was baptised on 12 June 1773 and the youngest, John, whose birth date was recorded as 7 September 1778, was baptised on 11 October that year.

Mary's parents were noted as always having 'maintained a reputable character', a familial attribute clearly not passed down to their daughter, as from an early age Mary was said to have displayed 'a knavish and vicious disposition'. At the age of five, it was reported that 'she stole a pair of morocco [fine leather] shoes, and secreted them for some months in her father's barn.' Later she brought them out and pretended she had found them; an inquiry proved that this was only one of those instances of lying which so strongly marked her future life. Whether the accounts of her early nefarious nature are to be believed, or whether at this tender age Mary could be forgiven for merely being a mischievous little girl, she did in her early years mix with the gypsies who habitually descended annually in great numbers for the Topley Fair – a sheep and horse fair that had been held at Topcliffe on 17–19 July since medieval times, and a traditional rendezvous for gypsies and horse-dealers from far and wide. The 'Egyptians' as the Elizabethans called them a century and a half earlier were the 'Moon Men', a dangerous mob of vagabonds who were by law to be driven out of parishes. They had come to be accepted by Mary's time, but no one quite trusted them.

Today the small village of Topcliffe is a quiet place, though still larger and busier than neighbouring Asenby, and it is hard to imagine that this ancient settlement was once an important town, staging one of the largest annual fairs in the north of England. The charter which allowed this fair, and a weekly market, was granted by Edward III in 1327. Some vestiges of Topcliffe's market square can still be seen, traces of where the stalls would have been pitched still apparent in the now narrow cordon of cobbles surrounding the Market Cross. While the sale of livestock was the primary concern, the first of the three successive days of the Fair was allotted for the sale of sheep and the second for horses. The third day was Lady Fair Day, for which the fair was renowned,when the lads would take their sweethearts around the trinket stalls. A kaleidoscope of sights and sounds, the fair attracted entertainers such as rope dancers, tumblers, acrobats, with the addition of food stalls, fortune tellers, freak shows, and musicians playing hurdy-gurdys and fiddles. Of course the ubiquitous pickpockets and prostitutes would have been there as well.

Though the Topley Fairs ceased in the late 1960s, they must have been similar affairs to the long standing but still extant Appleby Horse Fair held in Cumbria each June. Attracting ten to fifteen thousand

Gypsies and Travellers each year, who regard Appleby Fair as the most important date in their calendar, it remains one of the largest of their gatherings, as well as being a continuing source of controversy and complaint for the local residents. The past Topley gatherings would have been equally colourful occasions, with the opportunity for Romany families and friends to meet, to buy and sell horses, and for the young folk to find themselves husbands and wives; it was also the agreed time for enemies to settle old scores. It was customary and understood that every quarrel which had occurred during the year, no matter how trivial, had to be settled with a stand up fight at Topley Fair. And fights were continually in progress, often escalating into a general free-for-all, down Mill Bank, as well as bare knuckle bouts taking place alongside the riverbank – there was even a special arena set aside for the women to fight in, by the river on the Asenby side of the bridge. This long standing custom, and one that died hard, was doubtless fuelled by the 'bough houses' that came into existence on the fair days, during which time anyone could sell beer by licence, and where stout liquor was specially brewed for the consumption of customers 'invited' to the house for a drink, marked by green branches displayed above the doors, hence the name.

With the increased opportunity for those attending the fair to quench their thirst, along with the damage to crops and broken down fences along Park Road and Sykes Lane where the travellers set up camp, and raced their horses along the road 'frightening villagers in Asenby', this was the less than savoury environment in which the young and impressionable Mary may have picked up some of the gypsy arts and skills that she was later to utilise in a criminal career. It may have been the early exposure to gypsy fortune telling that formed the bedrock of Mary's criminal career. The gullible flocked to her, as they did to others, to buy potions and love draughts, easily convinced of her supernatural talents and the power of the charms she sold.

Other than the annual excitement of the Topley Fair, we can assume that Mary's childhood was no different to that of any girl growing up in rural north Yorkshire toward the close of the eighteenth century; running around the countryside with her brothers and sisters, perhaps over the old stone bridge spanning the Swale to Topcliffe, surrounded by farmland as it was. The freedom conferred by fine summer weather and long hours of daylight would have been precious before the year wore on and the candles were lit earlier and earlier along with the fires in the hearth. As a little girl, she would doubtless have been taught to clean and sew. Most rural cottages had a spinning wheel even if the families were not part of the 'putting out' system of Yorkshire woollens before the coming of the mills. In her spare time, Mary might even have played on the Maiden's Bower, the site of a supposed motte and bailey castle to the east of the village of Asenby, on top of which are the remains of one of England's mystical and forgotten turf mazes, and one of only ten rare medieval turf labyrinths in the country. The tradition of such turf mazes, convoluted paths cut into an area of short grass, is a very ancient one, and speculation as to the purpose of such mazes has thrown up various theories, one of which is that they were used by villagers for entertainment, particularly on high days and holidays such as May Day. Mary must also have been aware of the fable associated with the Maiden Bower maze, that on a summer's evening, if you happen upon the centre of the maze and kneel down and put your ear to the ground, you can hear the fairies singing.

Fairies aside, in her juvenile years, numerous 'frauds and falsehoods' seem to have been attributed to Mary, the extent of which caused her parents to place her in service with a family in Thirsk at the age of twelve in an attempt to mend their daughter's ways. Thirsk lies in the Vale of Mowbray and was undergoing extensive changes in Mary's day with a canal, never finished, adding to the chaos of the town. Domestic service was one of the few employment options open to unmarried girls and young women in the late eighteenth century and, in view of her youth, Mary would invariably have been employed as a 'maid of all work', at the very bottom rung of the household ladder. Despite this, we know from her subsequent criminal career that Mary was literate. This was unusual in an agricultural family, especially for a girl. The prevailing attitude at the time, considered sexist today, was that girls were not worth educating as they would always be subservient to men. It is possible that she was taught at Sunday School, but Robert Raikes' drive to improve the religious knowledge of the poor did not take off until 1780, by which time Mary was already in Thirsk.

She would have been living in modest quarters and working miserably long hours in return for the customary low wage paid for unskilled housework. Many domestic servants under the age of sixteen were unpaid, with bed and board being regarded as adequate recompense. Even if she did receive a salary it would not have been more than £1 a year. As the lowest order of servant, her work would have been hard; most houses had to be washed from top to bottom twice a week and staircases and entrances had to be scrubbed daily. Young maids like Mary would have shared the jobs of house-maid, kitchen maid and scullion. An almost continuous supply of water was required to keep the household clean as well as for ablutions and for the kitchen. There was no flush toilet and new-fangled inventions like piped water were the preserve of the urban rich so, many times a day, she would have staggered back with buckets filled from the nearest pump. Rising at five o'clock every morning, Mary would have cleaned the hearth and lit the kitchen fire and prepared the utensils for the cook to make breakfast if the household employed one. Otherwise this task may have fallen to her too in a more modest household. Before the family woke, she would have lit the fires in their bedrooms, and afterward emptied their chamber pots and fetched hot water for washing. While the family breakfasted, Mary would make the beds, put back the shutters, sweep the rooms, clean the grates and take the washstand water downstairs before clearing the breakfast plates and dishes, scouring the pans with a mixture of sand and soap and then start the round of laborious repetitive tasks of scraping the fireplaces and scrubbing, sweeping and dusting that would continue as the pattern of her day. Working hours would have been longer in summer because of the light, though in winter her day would still not be done until 7pm, and then only after all the pans had been scrubbed after dinner and the bedrooms prepared. Of necessity, clothes often had to be brushed and sponged daily as the streets were so filthy, and servants would also have been expected to launder, mend and sew. We can assume that Mary was at least a fair seamstress in view of one of her later employments.

A servant's duties might also encompass buying milk from the cows led by milkmaids into the town and shopping for provisions, though this might have proved a welcome break from a mistress who expected her servants to work like drones, all the time showing a meek obedience and deference whenever they encountered a member of the family, as well as accepting punishment submissively. Servants were beaten for laziness, untidiness, carelessness and insolence to their employer, or simply if their master or mistress were in a bad temper. Though we don't know into which household Mary was placed, nearly every household who could afford to employed servants. Their number was a symbol of social standing, with the aristocracy employing as many as fifty, while the middle classes might employ three or four. Those lower down the social scale perhaps employed only one.

Mary may well have been placed in one of the larger houses in the town, some six miles from her home in Asenby village, as Thirsk was experiencing growth as a busy market town at this time. Already the focus of trade for the scores of surrounding villages, and with an economy bolstered by the wool and linen industries, it was the building of the turnpike roads that led to the town becoming a staging post on the Royal Mail's Edinburgh to London run via York. The Mail stopped in Thirsk to change horses every afternoon at 4 o'clock while the 'Express', the 'Highflyer' and other famous coaches kept an equally punctual schedule on the routes from London, Edinburgh, Newcastle, Leeds and Darlington. With coaches calling at The Three Tuns, adapted for use as a coaching inn around 1740, and The Golden Fleece, one of the oldest coaching inns in England, the sound of the four-in-hands as they galloped into Thirsk market place, hoofs and wheels clattering on the cobbled stones must have been familiar to Mary, and she may even have been employed in one of these inns at some point, as her tenures of employment in Thirsk turned out to be various and brief.

While a high turnover rate of those in service existed due to innumerable grievances and disputes between domestics and their masters and mistresses, usually women could expect to continue working until marriage. Towards the close of the eighteenth century this was typically around the age of twenty-four or a little older. However, after several dismissals from households in Thirsk, quitting each situation under suspicious circumstances, perhaps for petty pilfering, Mary moved to York in 1787. The ancient Eboracum of the Romans, where the VI Legion was based, the city had become an important Viking centre (Jorvik) and was the seat of the Second Primate of England – the Archbishopric of York. It retained much of its medieval past in Mary's time but was easily the biggest place she would have seen in her life up to this point. This was a smart move – gaining employment in another house in Thirsk would have required a character reference; unresolved 'disputes' were a serious obstacle to gaining a future position, especially in a town where Mary's dubious employment history must have been known. Whether Mary was dismissed in each instance, or left of her own volition, she could have faced months of unemployment, and worse still, while those discharged by their employers were owed wages up to the date of dismissal, a servant who quit was owed nothing. Presumably through the guile which would later become a prominent character trait, Mary secured another position in service in York. Before the year was out she was again dismissed, for the theft of articles from her mistress, and departed in disgrace, and presumably in a hurry, as she left without her clothes or wages. Now aged twenty, Mary had been sacked from so many positions that no one in their right mind would employ her. Without hope of a reference, she shrewdly opted to move to Leeds where her dubious reputation was unknown.

In 1788, Leeds was a large town. Already described in 1730 as one of the 'largest and most flourishing towns in the country', with the momentum of the Industrial Revolution its expansion had continued. Typical of the rapidly growing manufacturing towns that had long been established as markets for the sale of cloth, Leeds had all the characteristics of the burgeoning industrial environment. By 1801, the year of the first census, the population of Leeds had reached 30,000, almost double that of York. This increase was caused by a rise in the birth rate and an influx of people looking for work; a labouring multitude who supplied the new urban mills and factories with cheap labour and worked hard. They drove the success of industrial Leeds, but nevertheless endured poverty, overcrowding and little if any prospect of improving their lot. Where better, then, for Mary to become lost in the anonymity of the swelling crowd? In time she could exploit the gullible weaknesses of the poor and desperate, easily deceived into placing their simple trust in the hands of a compulsive liar, confidence trickster, thief and fraudster, who through her skill as an accomplished actress could make her victims believe that she had supernatural powers. The fact that she could write must have immediately impressed her target group.

Though she remained without employment or friends for a considerable time, clearly Mary decided that joining the swelling ranks of factory workers was not for her, perhaps because she knew that the conditions in the factories were harsh. The work was very hard, and the hours long at up to seventy-two a week. Accidents were commonplace; exhausted factory hands carrying out repetitive tasks easily made mistakes, and with the absence of any health and safety precautions – there were usually no guards on the machinery – the work was also very dangerous. In some mills, especially in the flax mills which proliferated in Leeds where the flax spun was later woven into linen, the air was full of dust, creating and worsening many health conditions. There was also the risk of fire – the serious blaze which broke out in one Leeds flax mill will be covered in the following chapter. One young worker, James Carpenter, reported an horrific accident which happened to one of his colleagues at the mill he worked in:

> 'Harriet Wilson worked at Mr. Tennant's: her arms were taken off by the side gearing of a card, on the opposite side to where the straps run. I saw it done. She was picking the flyings off, just a little before 12 o'clock in the day; and the wheel caught her sleeve and pulled one arm in. In trying to extricate that the other went in.'

However, another determining factor in Mary not seeking such employment may well have been her age. Factory owners preferred to hire children because they were a cheaper source of labour than adults and easier to discipline. Children as young as nine were employed in the mills, though at one Leeds factory, Marshall & Co, older children of eleven or twelve were favoured, as they worked harder and did not have to be supervised.

Nevertheless, Mary needed to earn a living and there was another option open to her – many women believed that prostitution was less dangerous than factory work and more bearable than the back-breaking servility of domestic service. Young girls frequently took to the streets without understanding the inherent dangers of their new profession. Living a hand to mouth existence, pawning their clothes to buy drink – most prostitutes were addicted to gin within months of starting work. The majority would be beaten by their clients and in this situation, the girls' appeal to law would be pointless. Since most men in large cities had contracted venereal disease, nearly all working girls were infected within a year of walking the streets. Many turned to petty crime, and only those who stole from their clients broke even. If they escaped prosecution many died within five years from disease, assault by a client or as result of a botched abortion, a circumstance pertinent to Mary Bateman's later career. Yet the path to the streets was one which Mary didn't follow either. Instead, a friend of her mother got her a job in the shop of a mantua maker. This was a fashionable ladies over-gown of the period usually worn with a co-ordinating petticoat and it was here that Mary rather surprisingly remained for more than three years, obviously displaying some aptitude as a seamstress. If she was repeating her behavioural pattern of theft in stealing from this employer, Mary must have been very careful. But she began supplementing her earnings with a profitable side-line as a soothsayer, telling fortunes and making love potions for would-be sweethearts.

Mary's reputation as something of a 'witch' was not new, however. Another 'sorceress' hailing from Yorkshire, the Knaresborough-based Ursula Southill, better known as Mother Shipton, had been famed for prophesying the future some three centuries previously. She exhibited prophetic and psychic abilities from an early age and, with her large crooked nose, bent back and twisted legs, to the superstitious her appearance was that of the archetypal 'witch'. Though she was taunted by the local populace, they nevertheless bought her remedies and potions made from local flowers and herbs. Her prophecies began with seemingly insignificant premonitions, but as she practiced, her confidence grew and she became known as 'Knaresborough's Prophetess'. Earning her living by foretelling what the future held, when she spoke people believed her and passed her words on, and her power to see into the future made her well known not only in her hometown but throughout the country as a whole.

Mother Shipton lived in Tudor England but she predicted the fates of several monarchs in the future, not to mention the Great Fire of London in 1666, the building of the Crystal Palace in 1851 and the outbreak of the Crimean War in 1854.

While the infamous witch hunts that had reached their peak in Britain in the seventeenth century had long since abated (the last 'witch' to be executed in England was Alice Molland, who was sent to the gallows in Exeter in 1684) the decline in trials and hunts, the result of the Church's condemnation of witches as devil-worshipping heretics, did not necessarily mean a decline in the long held belief in witches, and unfounded fears and irrationality still abounded, even in the Age of Reason which saw the arrival of the steam engine and a certain intellectual opposition to superstition. Among the poor there was still the dread of the unknown. Trust in magic or chance was commonplace and Mary Bateman was well placed to exploit this fear in the susceptible souls amongst the poor and dispossessed now inhabiting the rapidly growing town of Leeds.

For these people, living conditions were grim. Wages were very low; men rarely earned more than twelve shillings a week, women only two or three shillings. Children got half of that again but in many cases their addition to the family income was vital. From these meagre earnings, as well as food, there were basics like candles, salt, fuel, clothes and linen that had to be paid for, and then there was the rent.

Families were crammed into the first developments of 'blind back' houses, the precursors of back-to-back housing, built around yards and courts behind the main streets of the town. As their fronts faced each other across a small courtyard and adjacent properties were similarly developed, the blind back houses became back-to-backs. Scantily furnished with few possessions, except for some basic furniture and cooking utensils, the space would have been inevitably cramped in the face of economic necessity and the absence of any effective birth control. Many were close to destitution in a climate of overcrowding and deprivation, living in filthy conditions where dysentery outbreaks were frequent. Mary played on the superstition of this first and second generation of mill workers. She used the old wives' tales that it was risking lifelong spinsterhood to sit on a table; that to rock an empty cradle would encourage the birth of another child. And she almost certainly began to add abortion to her repertoire.

Two other 'witches' were operating in Yorkshire at the time. One was 'Old Nan', the locally renowned 'cunning woman' who lived beneath the overhang of Kilnsey Crag in Wharfedale in the late 1700s. Old Nan, or Nancy Winter to give her real name, was famous throughout the Craven district for telling people's fortunes, and even had a witchcraft 'shop' in Bag's Alley in Skipton. How effective her predictions were remains questionable in view of the fact that 'her stock of spells was not very large'. Old Nan relied on her pet guinea pig and half a pack of dirty playing cards in divining futures. The other was Hannah Green, or the 'Ling Bob Witch' as she was commonly known. A renowned fortune teller who lived on the outskirts of Bradford in the latter half of the 18th century, she must have been very successful as by the time she died in 1810 she had saved more than £1,000, a fortune at the time. Her chosen method of divination was the reading of tea leaves, a popular method of fortune telling which began to increase in popularity during the seventeenth century when tea was introduced into Europe from China, although she could occasionally be induced to make more general prophecies. The services of the Ling Bob Witch came to be held in such high esteem that the rich and aristocratic would travel considerable distances for a consultation, their carriages with teams of horses and attendant grooms not an uncommon sight, often seen lined up outside her home. This was a cottage on the edge of the moor on the left of the old road from Otley to Bradford, between Carlton and Yeadon, the tall chimney stack painted white so her gentrified clients would know where to find her. Clearly Old Nan and the Ling Bob Witch, whose career spanned forty years, were rather more benign practitioners than Mary Bateman. No whiff of any criminal association ever attached itself to either of them. It was said that, after nightfall, Hannah Green could transform herself into any form, but both she and Nancy Winter were free of the accusations of frauds, petty thefts, poisonings and murder that were to cling to Mary.

Interestingly, the village of Mary's birth also spawned another who 'was looked upon by some as a witch', a woman called Peggy Lumley who lived in Asenby in the mid-1800s. A description of Peggy was given by T Carter Mitchell in the *Thirsk Falcon* (1887–1891), a magazine written for the Masonic Lodge of the same name, though Carter Mitchell himself was a noted local personality, known for donning his frock coat and top hat on the first evening of the Topley Fair and making his way down the hill and over the bridge to the gypsy encampment where he visited each caravan and welcomed the occupants. His portrayal of Peggy Lumley ran thus:

> 'A great reader, especially of quaint old books which taught of necromancy and magic art. A clever, strong-minded woman, she mingled her conversations with dark sayings too deep for the comprehension of her associates ... Her appearance too was striking. A tall commanding figure she reminded one of the

> enchantress Medea but for a fearsome squint in her eyes which, although it detracted from her comeliness, became well a votary of the "black art". There were even stories circulating 'of persons who, having unwittingly angered Peggy, received from her a look which made them return home with foreboding to find some of their stock stone-dead.'

Clearly, Peggy Lumley was a force to be reckoned with and she should certainly not be crossed. Perhaps it was something in Asenby's water!

In late 1792, Mary was still working in the shop of the mantua-maker. The soothsaying side-line had expanded, and as many folk believed her to possess supernatural powers of divination and fortune-telling, the smooth-tongued deceiver gained something of a reputation amongst the superstitious of Leeds. In addition to telling fortunes, she specialised in the 'removal of evil wishes', but unlike the Ling Bob Witch's affluent customer base, drew her clientele largely from the ranks of servant girls who occasionally introduced their mistresses to Mary's services.

At the age of twenty-four, Mary seems also to have cast another kind of spell with a view to her longer term prospects – bewitching a potential source of livelihood and security in the shape of one John Bateman. Bateman was a wheelwright, the son of another John Bateman who was the Town Crier of Thirsk. Astonishingly, after a whirlwind courtship of only three weeks, the couple were married by licence at St Peter's Church, Leeds, on 26 February 1793.

But marriage did nothing to change Mary Harker's old ways. Within two months of the newly-weds moving into furnished lodgings in High Court Lane, close to the river wharves and just west of the parish church where they had married, Mary had already stolen from another lodger on the premises. Breaking open the man's box of belongings, she stole his watch, some silver spoons and two guineas.

In this instance, Mary escaped prosecution and the full weight of the law by returning the stolen goods and cash; 'there can be little doubt,' *The Extraordinary Life* acerbically recorded, 'that the young man who she robbed made her infamy the price of his clemency'. Returning the stolen goods was a tactic that Mary would later repeatedly employ to escape prosecution. When the Batemans later took in lodgers of their own, a Mr Dixon found that he frequently missed small sums of money kept in his room. In total, two guineas was found to have disappeared. The finger of suspicion firmly pointed to Mary, and despite her protestations of innocence, Mr Dixon's threats of prosecution induced Mary to 'hush up the disgraceful business by returning his money'. This was a clever move on Mary's part as at the time the statute books legislated that the theft of more than forty shillings from a dwelling place – twenty-one shillings making up a guinea – was a capital offence. Incidentally, pickpocketing more than a shilling on the street and the theft of five shillings from a shop also carried the same penalty. This heavy-handed overuse of punishment did not end until the reform of the penal code by Robert Peel, Home Secretary in the 1820s.

Though Mary managed to escape the implications of her discovered thefts, it seems she turned to the less direct method of 'appropriation in fraudulently obtaining retail goods', which could then presumably be sold on. In the eighteenth century, it was common for shopkeepers to allow customers to buy items on credit, or 'on account' with no money exchanged up-front. Posing as a buyer for a 'Miss Stephenson' Mary went shopping. Calling at a linen draper's shop in Leeds, she asked for fabrics to make up into three silk petticoats, in the fictitious customer's name, to be sent for Miss Stephenson's inspection. Upon Miss Stephenson's selection, two of the petticoats would be returned to the shop and the third kept and paid for. Indeed, two articles were returned. But Mary kept the third, directing that it should be charged to Miss Stephenson's account. Of course it was never paid for, and the out of pocket draper was left with egg on his face. Mary was further successful in getting her hands on 'a gown-piece and two webs of cloth' as well as some flannel fabric, but this time using the name 'Mrs Smith' to dupe another unsuspecting shopkeeper. It is a testament to Mary's skill as an actress that in spite of the several charges of swindling that were levelled against her, the shopkeepers involved were persuaded into a mistaken clemency and forgave her. In hindsight, had they not been so kind, the lives of many unfortunate people might have escaped ruin.

Obviously, Mary's darkening reputation meant that a frequent change of address was a shrewd and necessary move. A little over a year after their marriage, the Batemans moved from High Court Lane and took a house in the yard of a Mr Wells, a spirit merchant who lived on Briggate, then as now at the heart of Leeds shopping centre and about a third of a mile from where the Batemans had previously lived, a safe enough remove from their previous lodgings. While the accommodation in High Court Lane had been furnished, the couple apparently furnished their new abode in Well's Yard themselves in 'a tolerable comfortable manner', possibly financed by Mary's various thefts and scams, many of which must have gone unnoticed and unrecorded. In these first years of industrialisation, the flotsam of mill workers drifted constantly. No one of Mary's class could afford their own homes, so they rented, often from unscrupulous landlords out to rook them. Unable to afford the rent, tenants sublet and the subtenants did likewise, so that tenements filled up with anonymous people who came and went on a regular basis.

Whether John Bateman was either unaware or unwilling to acknowledge the truth, he cannot have failed to notice the pattern of accusations of theft that appeared to dog his wife. But what Mary did next must surely have sharpened any suspicions John Bateman harboured about the audacity and wickedness of the character of the woman that he had married.

Chapter 2

Mrs Moore's Screws

While Mary was busy with her various dupes, thefts and scams, her husband John was earning his rather more honest living as a wheelwright. He was employed in the business of the aptly named Mr Wright whose workshop, as listed in the Leeds Trade Directory covering the period 1790–1799, was located opposite the now demolished St James's Church in New York Street near Kirkgate Market. In fact, it was Wright who would later testify at Mary's trial as a crucial witness of the authentication of her handwriting, but here we are jumping ahead of her story.

John Bateman would have had a five minute walk to work from their lodgings in Wells' Yard, though it may sometimes have taken longer as the streets would have been busier on Tuesdays and Saturdays, the days of the twice weekly cloth market. This business had formerly been conducted on the Leeds Bridge, but the increase in manufacturers soon made the market too big to be confined to the bridge, so trading moved to the high street – Briggate – the wide road from the river crossing originally called Bridge Gate. The cloth market, which would eventually move to the Kirkgate site in 1822, began from the bridge, running along Briggate, at this time still lined with the old timber framed houses and the numerous shops and workshops which occupied the yards beyond, one of which of course belonged to the Bateman's landlord. It then followed the course of the street northward, almost to the Moot Hall at the Kirkgate junction with Commercial Street. Once adorned with a statue of Queen Anne, the Hall was the meeting place for the justices of the town and was also used to administer relief to the poor and determine the paternity of illegitimate children. It was where vagabonds were flogged; outside the front of the building were the pillory and stocks, and in 1664 the heads of three of the Farnley Wood plotters, anti-monarchists who planned to overthrow the recently restored Charles II – Robert Atkins, John Errington and Henry Wilson – were stuck on poles there, where they remained for thirteen years before being dislodged in a storm.

The area around the Moot Hall had long been subject to serious congestion; part of a block of buildings known as Middle Row. The ground floor below the courthouse was occupied by butcher's shops, and with a roadway on each side so narrow that it was dangerous for two carriages to pass one another. Although the original seventeenth century building was replaced in 1710, it was still considered a hindrance to traffic. Briggate was the general market place for the town, with cattle, fish and fruit for sale, with as much as five hundred loads of apples being sold in one day. John Bateman would have been part of the daily ebb and flow of the tide of pedestrian and wheeled traffic, though Mary herself would one morning contribute to the throng when, astutely timed after the arrival of the first post, she hurried to her husband's workplace, overwrought with feigned sorrow carrying a forged letter with the news that John's father, the resident Town Cryer of Thirsk, was near death.

Mary needn't have waited long to start out on her deceitful journey; the Post Office in nearby Boar Lane opened at eight o'clock in the morning in the winter months and seven in summer for the delivery of letters, 'and the letter carrier begins to deliver the letters in the town about the same time'. Of course, this was immaterial to Mary, as the forged letter she was delivering had never seen the inside of a post satchel. Arriving at Wright's workshop clutching the forgery detailing John Bateman Senior's imminent death, she entreated her husband that if he wanted to see his father before it was too late, he should immediately get to Thirsk to be by his father's side. Understandably distraught, John downed tools, and, borrowing a small amount of money from his understanding employer to cover travelling expenses, he started out on the near forty-mile journey to Thirsk. Whether John hired a hack and rode there or caught one of the many mail coaches which left Leeds daily or whether he begged rides along the way we do not know. Delivery waggons are mentioned in the Leeds Directory (R Sweeting's waggons setting off from the Call Lane warehouse ran a route to Stockton via Thirsk) so this would be a possibility. When John arrived in the town he must have been astonished and relieved, to see his father alive and well and ringing his bell, crying the news in Thirsk town square. 'I am glad' said the bewildered son to his father 'to see you so much better.' 'Better?' said his perplexed father, 'nothing has ailed me.' It now became clear that the dire contents of the letter which Mary had so hurriedly borne to her husband was a wicked lie on his wife's part, and when the furious husband returned to Leeds, her motive became all too apparent. During John's engineered absence, Mary had sold every belonging and stick of furniture from their rented house and used the monies presumably to pay off the victim, or victims, of another of her thefts.

We must assume that in spite of his wife's outrageous behaviour, forgiveness was in John Bateman's nature, and that the couple were reconciled after this incident, at least periodically, as their marriage produced three children – possibly as many as five. The article appearing in the *Leeds Mercury* detailing Mary's arrest in October 1808 noted that she was the mother of 'several children'. The paper was a prominent local weekly with a readership of 3,000. It cost 6d because of the increased stamp duty and its editor was Edward Baines. We know that the Batemans had a son called Jack as mention was made of him at Mary's trial, and presumably this child was the same John Bateman

(Jack being a traditional diminutive for John), who was baptised on 21 February 1796 in St Peter's Parish Church, where his parents had been married, the paternal relationship noted in the baptismal register as 'Father: John Bateman'. The church is Leeds Minster today. The vicar who baptised John was Peter Haddon. The same records yield the earlier baptism of a Mary Bateman, noted as daughter of John Bateman, on 16 February 1794, a little less than a year after Mary and John's marriage, and possibly the daughter that Mary referred to in a letter written to her husband from the condemned cell at York Castle Gaol, requesting that her wedding ring be bequeathed to the child, a traditional bequest as the girl, named for her mother, was the eldest. Records of Mary's last days also indicate that she was allowed to have her youngest child, although the sex wasn't stipulated, with her in the condemned cell until her execution – this may have been James Bateman, again recorded as the son of John Bateman, who was baptised at St Peter's on 19 July 1807. The register of St Peter's also show records for the baptisms of a Maria Bateman on 6 December 1801 and George Bateman baptised on 20 May 1804, and as both births fall neatly into the obstetric gap between the births of the eldest child Mary, and James born in the summer of 1807, Maria and George may well have been the elder siblings of James who is the most likely candidate for the child sharing Mary's imprisonment. The child would still have been classed as care-dependant of a nursing mother – young children cared for by their mothers in prison being a distressing yet common practice.

John Bateman, nevertheless, must have had serious reservations about leaving his wife to her own devices for any length of time, as in an encore to the house-clearance she had previously performed during John's mercy dash to his 'dying' father's side, when he was next absent visiting friends, Mary took the opportunity to sell all of her husband's clothes, as well as many other of his belongings, along with some items she had stolen from a neighbouring tailor's shop.

We cannot know what exactly made Mary tick. Did she steal for the vicarious excitement? The risk of getting caught? Or was she merely a plain opportunist stealing purely for profit or greed? The issues of compulsive criminal behaviours have only relatively recently been identified and classified as mental health conditions. This aspect of Mary's life is examined more closely in the last chapter. That Mary felt no compunction regarding her actions however is obvious, and her next fraudulent endeavour was indeed shameless.

On 13 February 1796, a serious fire broke out in the Marshall & Benyon flax mill in Water Lane, in the industrial district of Holbeck on the western outskirts of Leeds. During the eighteenth century, fires were commonplace in mills, with the processing of flax creating a highly combustible dust, and the risk exacerbated by hot machine bearings lubricated with linseed oil, as well as the additional risk posed by workers using candles. Needless to say, the catastrophe was compounded by the inadequacies of fire-fighting capabilities at this time – hand drawn manual pumps with a short range were the only equipment available. For most of the eighteenth century, individual insurance companies maintained their own fire brigades, extinguishing fires only in those buildings insured by the company providing fire cover. It was not until the mid-1850s that the first reliable steam powered appliances were adopted by brigades.

This particular mill fire not only resulted in crushing financial costs amounting to £10,000 – in the region of 6 million pounds by today's reckoning – only half of which was met by the insurance, but also tragically brought a cost in lives as ten people were known to have died in the blaze when one of the walls collapsed.

With sympathies amongst the townsfolk running high for the injured and bereaved, Mary saw an opportunity to make good on the tragedy. Without a shred of genuine contrition, she set about 'relief' work in collecting sheets from charitable souls for the purposes of laying out the dead whose relations were too poor to meet the cost themselves, initially playing on the goodwill of a Miss Maude, a lady known for her 'humane disposition'. She had been charitably moved to supply Mary with sheets to wrap the body of a child who had fallen victim in the mill fire, and whose mother was too impoverished to provide the necessary linen herself. However, the sheets acquired by Mary, along with linen begged from three other good hearted benefactors, ended up pledged in the pawnbrokers. Pawn shops, their three-ball signs a reminder of an illiterate age, sprang up wherever the working class congregated. It was possible to 'pledge' an item in exchange for instant cash, said item to be redeemed when financial times were easier. Pawnbrokers were often 'fences' of stolen goods and few of them asked searching questions.

Yet the mileage Mary exacted from this calamity didn't end here, as she further had the audacity to pose as a nurse from the Leeds General Infirmary, and in this guise was successful in collecting even more linen on the pretext that it was needed to dress the wounds of those lying injured in the infirmary. Before Florence Nightingale made nursing a respectable, middle-class vocation in the 1850s, 'nurses' were often prostitutes who provided comforts to male patients that would never be available on today's NHS! Hospitals themselves were unhygienic in Mary's day, spreading the very diseases they were supposed to be dealing with. Leeds General was built in 1771 where today's Yorkshire Bank stands off City Square. Its founding doctors were all graduates of the University of Edinburgh Medical School. Of course, the reality was that Mary pawned this linen too.

Whether or not John Bateman had been turning a blind eye to his wife's deceits, the time came when he could no longer live in a state of denial, and in order to escape the inevitable derision and possible legal ramifications of Mary's frauds, he decided to join the supplementary militia to get out of Leeds, away from the disgrace caused by his wife's conduct, and the stigma that must now have been attached to the name of Bateman in many quarters.

The militia were a vital part of homeland defences in the late eighteenth and early nineteenth centuries, aimed at creating a professional national military reserve, and embodied at various times during the French and Napoleonic Wars (1792–1815). They served at several strategic locations, particularly stationed on the South Coast and in Ireland. Both these areas were highly vulnerable. In the 1790s and again in 1804, the French had active plans in place to invade the coast of Sussex and Kent. Ireland had for centuries been a hotbed of anti-English violence, culminating in an attempt by the revolutionary Wolfe Tone and his United Irishmen to encourage a French invasion of England. This was famously dispersed by a handful of Welsh fishwives at Fishguard, Pembrokeshire, in 1798. Men were selected by ballot to serve for longer periods, but volunteers also came forward to fill the militia quotas, as was the case with John Bateman. This civilian force, whose officers consisted of local gentlemen, drew their ranks from the poor and semi-literate, and the wives of those men already married were allowed to live within the walls of the garrison and follow their husbands wherever they might be stationed. Whether willingly or not, John took Mary with him, and in doing so exposed his wife to a whole new sphere of opportunity in which to expand her nefarious activities.

While on the march, encamped, in barracks or billeted in towns, naturally the militia were closely engaged with the civilian population, and needless to say, trading relationships offering the opportunity for black market transactions in regimental clothing and equipment were many. Mary would soon have had her fingers firmly stuck into one of the many illegal 'pies' afforded her. Of course, her new situation would also have considerably widened Mary's scope for the performance of her established arts of fortune telling and divination, capitalising on the gullible and unsuspecting within the ranks, as well as the people of the districts wherever the regiment ended up. Married quarters for Other Ranks offered little privacy. Beds were arranged in dormitories, the family 'home' being a bed on the other side of a horse blanket slung over a rope across the room.

No specific details of Mary's exploits during her husband's service have come down to us, but it is safe to assume that she got up to her old tricks and maybe even acquired some new ones. Eventually, and perhaps again of necessity, after three years, John quitted the service and in 1799 the couple returned to Leeds, perhaps feeling that enough time had passed for the outrage and memory of Mary's prior misdemeanours and blackened reputation in that town to have sufficiently faded.

Taking up residence in Marsh Lane, near Timble Bridge, and a good half mile from their previous home in Wells' Yard, Mary set up selling trinkets and love charms and offering her healing services and predictions of the future to unsuspecting customers taken in by her guile. Regardless of Mary's proficiency, whether her clients were satisfied by a coincidental happy chance outcome, or conversely were too ashamed to admit they'd resorted to Mary's ministrations if the matter did not turn out well for them, at this time Mary began to specialise as a professional agent for a 'screwer-down', an art which requires some explanation.

Persuasive in convincing her victims that someone or other intended them harm, Mary nevertheless assured them that the potential evil-doer could be prevented from acting if they were 'screwed down'. While Mary did not profess to be able to perform this service herself, she would defer in such matters to a certain 'Mrs Moore', a respectable name for Mary's entirely fictitious colleague who possessed supernatural skills as the seventh child of a seventh child. The number seven had ancient magical properties or so the superstitious believed. The seventh child of a seventh child was particularly blessed with second sight. Intriguingly, some believed that such an offspring was the agent of the Devil. Mary would seek Mrs Moore's counsel for those knottier problems she felt herself unable to resolve; Mrs Moore was apparently proficient as a screwer-down of husbands with wandering affections and equally adept and much employed as a screwer-down of creditors pursuing unpaid debts, with Mary acting as her agent, and of course taking payment on the lady's behalf. It was while acting as Mrs Moore's representative that Mary also started a business as a part-time abortionist.

While procuring or performing abortion was against the law – prior to 1803, abortion or the offence of 'attempting to induce a miscarriage' was punishable by a fine or short term of imprisonment – as the population of Leeds continued to swell, so too did the birth rate. In such a climate of poverty and overcrowding, and in the absence of any effective methods of birth control, Mary's services must have been in demand. For those in desperate and dire straits, the alternative was infanticide, a crime for which a woman could be found guilty, under a statute passed in 1624, even if she simply tried to hide her pregnancy and later miscarried, or if the infant was stillborn. Understandably, countless women sought to remedy their condition, especially amongst the ranks of domestic servants who often stood to lose their position if they were discovered to be with child. Single teenage girls, recent migrants to the city in fruitless search of work as domestic servants accounted for about a third of those who turned to working the streets of Leeds as prostitutes, and there were many like Mary herself on hand to offer their services, for monetary gain of course. Her knowledge of folk remedies, of harvesting and administering the centuries old concoctions of Pennyroyal and Tansy, and the most effective combinations of these herbal abortifacients had most probably been garnered from the Topley Fair gypsies with whom Mary had so freely mingled in her childhood. Pennyroyal (*mentha pulegium*) also called puddling grass smells of spearmint and is highly toxic. In small doses it was used in cooking and the making of herbal tea. Tansy (*tanacetum vulgare*) also called bitter buttons, was used to *aid* conception as well as induce abortions.

Nevertheless, there was a high risk of endangering the life of the mother, as attested to by the many murder cases in the late eighteenth and early nineteenth centuries that were a consequence of poisonous draughts administered in an attempt to induce an abortion. We do not know how many of the women that Mary 'helped out' suffered fatal consequences, but Mary certainly supplied something stronger than a 'herbal remedy' to at least one young woman as detailed later in this chapter.

With regard to the mysterious Mrs Moore, a lady called Mrs Greenwood was the first recorded victim of Mary's dupe, though many had probably preceded her. Mary had obviously identified Mrs Greenwood as susceptible, and manipulated the poor woman into believing that she had foreseen a terrible future for her. Mrs Greenwood, she predicted, was in danger of attempting suicide in view of the desperate domestic misfortunes about to befall her, namely that her husband, who was away from home at the time, had been locked up in jail and that only Mrs Moore could secure his release. According to Mary, four guards had been set to watch over Mr Greenwood in his imprisonment, and the necessary course of action would be to screw down the guards to facilitate his escape. As there were four of them, in order for Mrs Moore to get Greenwood out, Mrs Greenwood would need to provide four pieces of leather, four pieces of blotting paper, four brass screws and, tellingly, four pieces of gold to make an effective charm. The window of opportunity was narrow however, and if these items were not placed in Mary's hands by nightfall, by the following morning Mrs Greenwood would be a widow. While Mrs Greenwood may well have been able to get the first three items on the list, she certainly didn't have four pieces of gold, yet Mary had a ready suggestion to overcome the obstacle; Mrs Greenwood could either borrow or steal the necessary coin. Fortunately for Mrs Greenwood, this last suggestion set alarm bells ringing, and the mention of theft brought her to her senses. Realising she had very nearly been taken in by Mary, she disassociated herself from the whole sorry affair, and was certainly the richer and hopefully the wiser for it. Sadly, in a testament to Mary's skill as a fraudster, many others were completely taken in.

Indeed, the next victims exposed to the Mrs Moore scenario proved more pliant, and in the Stead family Mary found ripe pickings in both husband and wife. Barzillai Stead, as a failed businessman, was easily persuaded that his creditors were fast closing in. With Mary succeeding in working his paranoia into panic, rather than face the inevitability of the bailiffs at his door, he decided to join the army, even handing over his enlistment fee to Mary. Recruits at the time received the 'king's shilling', the daily pay of an infantryman, but this was merely a token of signing on in an illiterate age. The 'bringer' or recruiting sergeant, as well as telling tall tales of regimental glory, would give the recruit a 'bounty' (additional expenses) which could add up to £9, more money than many men had seen before in their lives. This was removed from them for 'incidentals' when they reached the barracks and was probably the fee that Stead gave to Mary.

Simultaneously Mary worked on his wife, telling her that her husband was keeping a mistress, and that he was on the point of eloping with her when he left to join his regiment. The mistress, Mary said, lived in Vicar Lane, about half a mile further into the heart of Leeds and at the time an area crowded with slums and slaughterhouses. To add more fuel to the lie, the woman was also pregnant by Stead. The remedy for the situation would be for Mrs Moore to screw down the love rival, but in order to do so payment of three crowns was necessary – over a week's wages for a skilled craftsman – and Mrs Moore's screws would never drive without money. In addition to the cash fee, bizarrely, two pieces of coal were also required. Of course the money went straight into Mary's pocket, but the coal was to be placed on the mistress's doorstep, the idea being that upon discovery the pieces of coal would be thrown onto her fire, the smoke from which, after putting the love rival into a deep sleep would then taint all of her clothes freshly laundered in anticipation of the elopement. Mary reasoned that the mistress would be prevented from leaving with the errant husband as she would have no clean clothes to take with her. To all intents and purposes, from Mrs Stead's point of view, the charm worked; her husband left the next morning to join his regiment, without the mistress, who of course had never existed, and conveniently, his departure left his grateful and impressionable wife to the mercies of Mary, who proceeded to fleece her to the extent that she was forced to pawn virtually every article in the marital home. Eventually reduced to complete penury, she attempted suicide by drowning herself in the river Calder but was luckily saved. Mary's actions were rendered even more wicked in light of the fact that Mrs Stead was expecting a child.

At some point, the Leeds Benevolent Society intervened. This charity was also known as the Stranger's Friend Society, founded in 1789 by a group associated with the Wesleyan Methodist church. It investigated all applications for relief, gave food and money, found others work and provided children with a suitable education. Mrs Stead clearly qualified for assistance, and to ease the expectant mother's destitute situation, a guinea was offered in poor relief, paid in three separate payments of seven shillings. Mary, however, managed to extort eighteen shillings of the relief payment, to be used to screw down the Benevolent Society into granting further monies on the wretched woman's behalf. In her desperate and highly susceptible state, Mary also convinced Mrs Stead that it was the intention of her father-in-law to murder her. Naturally it was only Mrs Moore who possessed the power to avert the crime, though a further guinea would be required in payment. Pawning what few possessions she had left to raise the sum, Mrs Stead was nevertheless safe in the knowledge that Mrs Moore's ministrations had paid off – after all, her father-in-law had made no attempt on her life.

Even though Mrs Stead had virtually nothing left, Mary continued to put pressure on the poor woman. She told her that the Steads' daughter, eight at the time, would become pregnant at fourteen and would either 'murder herself' or be murdered by her seducer. The solution was for the child to wear a silver charm bracelet. That would keep her safe but would cost seventeen shillings, to be paid to Mrs Moore. Needless to say, Mary switched the silver, and the charm was later discovered to be made of pewter. This falsehood, along with the many others perpetrated by Mary were finally exposed when one of Mrs Stead's neighbours managed to convince the distraught woman that she had been utterly taken in. By this time, the few tools left behind by her husband before he joined the army, and the only items now left in the house, were pawned in payment for screwing down all the officers in his regiment with a view to securing his discharge. It was possible to buy one's way out of the army, but the cost was huge. Oddly enough, in this instance Mrs Moore's ministrations failed, perhaps as there was now nothing left to extort.

Having wrung this victim dry, Mary turned her attention to a young relative of the Steads who had come to Leeds when she'd found herself pregnant and deserted by the father. Mary assured the young woman that the purchase of a series of charms, priced at one guinea each, would bring the baby's errant father to her side. When the magic failed, Mary then promised to ensnare the eligible son of a reasonably affluent family for whom the girl had worked in service. With no proposal forthcoming, Mary recommended a stronger charm, at additional cost of course. When this also failed, she offered, and presumably at additional cost again, to provide medicines that would induce an abortion.

The concoctions did indeed work, but also wrecked the health of the young woman, who, in an advanced state of emaciation exclaimed, 'Had I never known Mary Bateman, my child would now have been in my arms, and I should have been a healthy woman – but it is in eternity, and I am going after it as fast as time and a ruined constitution can carry me.' Whether the death of this unfortunate young woman and her unborn child were the first directly attributable to the ministrations of Mary as an abortionist we cannot now know. The only redeeming feature of the whole Stead affair was that eventually Mary was exposed – though Mrs Stead still fervently believed that the charms stitched into her clothing had the power to preserve her life. These were merely a number of long strips of paper tied in a knot enclosing a small scrap of rag and a small piece of gilt leather. When she was eventually persuaded to remove them, upon finding she was still well and breathing, the awful realisation of Mary's exploitation of herself and her family led the wronged woman to threaten Mary with arrest and imprisonment for fraud, unless she immediately redeemed all the pawned household items and made good on the money she had extorted. Realising the game was up, Mary repaid the sum of four guineas, which we must assume was not honestly come by, but as for returning Mrs Stead's furniture and clothing, unsurprisingly she reneged on her word. Yet it is a testament to Mary's skill as a consummate deceiver that she continued to find a flourishing market for her criminal 'services', though it was possibly Mary's next mark, a family called Cooper, that funded the repayment of the four guineas as she undoubtedly ran her scams concurrently.

Whether or not the Coopers were aware of Mary's infamy, Mrs Cooper was nevertheless persuaded, through ignorance or blind faith, to believe that her husband was intent on selling the contents of their home and deserting with the proceeds. To avoid this and being left destitute, Mrs Cooper was advised by Mary to lodge the best of her furniture in Mary's house for safe-keeping, including a fine grandfather clock, which very soon ended up in the pawnbrokers, along with the rest of the Coopers' belongings. At least the Coopers emerged from their dealings with Mary with their lives, which is more than can be said for the three unfortunate women, a mother and two daughters, who ended up buried in the same grave, a consequence of Mary's evil enterprise. This time, there was another alter ego – enter Miss Blythe.

Chapter 3

From The Hand Of Miss Blythe

As a precursor to the poisoning for which Mary Bateman was eventually to be tried and hanged, the Misses Kitchin, two unmarried Quaker sisters who ran a small drapers shop with their mother near St Peter's Square in Leeds, certainly had cause to rue their acquaintance with Mary. St Peter's Square fell within the Quarry Hill district of Leeds, in Georgian times a fashionable and genteel spa area where people came to take the benefit of the waters. From the seventeenth century, the northern spa resorts of Harrogate, Ilkley and the area around Croft-on-Tees were better known for offering a variety of hydro and other therapies, usually rather high-class affairs with residential accommodation. Leeds also began to exploit its own spas owing to the sulphuric waters bubbling up from the underlying geology, but although the waters from St Peter's Well were said to ward off rheumatism and rickets, the sulphuric waters were also a contributory factor in the development of Leeds' tanning and dyeing industries.

After ingratiating herself with the Kitchin sisters, Mary sometimes worked in their shop, becoming a confidante of theirs. As many had done before, and would continue to do, the ladies fell for Mary's special brand of mysticism in predicting their futures. Although we cannot say to what extent the Kitchin sisters were staunch Quakers, it may be testament to Mary's powers of persuasion that she duped them at all, since White magic, no less than Black, was condemned by Members of the Society of Friends. Some early Quakers were particularly vocal against the practices of 'cunning folk', perhaps because they themselves were accused by their critics of using sorcery to attract new members to their faith, and so wanted to distance themselves from such practices. Indeed, the final line of *The Extraordinary Life* sermonises that 'Those who trust in *Diviners* shall be confounded and perish'. Perhaps however, the Kitchin sisters were more amenable to prophecies passed on from a third party, as Mary's predictions now came from the successor to Mrs Moore, the equally fictitious 'Miss Blythe' whom Mary, as her mouthpiece, confidently asserted had the power to divine destinies. Why Mary decided to switch alter egos at this point is a mystery, though Miss Blythe, who apparently lived in Scarborough, was a true proficient and able to 'read the stars'. Scarborough had been an important medieval stronghold (its castle ruins still dominate the skyline) but the acidic waters discovered by Elizabeth Farrow in 1626 had led to the place becoming a spa town. By 1735, it had new-fangled bathing machines that could be rolled down the beach to the water's edge. Its elevation to a spa town gave Scarborough a new gentility which may well have impressed the Misses Kitchin.

In early September 1803 one of the sisters fell ill. Whether her sickness was genuine or induced by Mary we can only guess and Mary, in feigned concern, took upon herself the task of nursing her. Mary also had the kindness of heart to get medicines for her patient, apparently obtained directly from the hand of Miss Blythe, and personally prepared and administered these powders. Within a week, Miss Kitchin was dead. On hearing of her daughter's precarious health, the girl's mother had hurried to Leeds from Wakefield to be by her side, and though Mrs Kitchin had been in perfect health when she embarked on her journey, within days of her arrival both the mother and the surviving daughter appeared to be stricken with the same symptoms of the fatal illness. Just ten days after the first Miss Kitchin had taken a turn for the worse, all three of the women were dead, and at the time the cause of death was attributed to cholera morbus, a disease that was not yet fully understood and which would not hit Britain as a pandemic until 1831.

Pertinent to Mary's methods, before the development of analytical chemistry increasing the risk that a poisoner would be caught, poison was a popular method of murder. A modus operando frequently employed by females, requiring no physical exertion, the lady of the house was also ideally placed to conveniently administer a poison as they were predominantly involved with the preparation of food and the management of, and access to household remedies and 'medicines'. In Mary's case, the administration of the poison which killed the first Kitchin sister was rendered all the more convenient as she dosed her under the confident belief that a remedy was being given.

It would seem, from the symptoms of the victims, that Mary was indeed using arsenic. From the close of the eighteenth century arsenic pervaded almost every aspect of everyday life in Britain, and the poison left a hefty toll of death and debilitation. As a by-product of an emerging smelting industry, it was cheap and readily available as a rat killer by the early 1800s. Though it later became *the* poison of choice in Victorian melodrama and the popular press, a significant proportion of the fatalities caused by arsenic were more pedestrian, resulting from accidental use in food. Arsenic was virtually odourless and tasteless and easily confused with flour or sugar and other cooking essentials. Two cases long after Mary Bateman highlight the problem. In November of 1858 the 'Bradford Humbug Poisoning' had resulted in the accidental arsenic poisoning of more than 200 people when sweets inadvertently made with arsenic were sold from a market stall. A pharmacist's assistant had accidentally sold arsenic trioxide in place of the harmless calcium sulphate and the terrible results spoke for themselves.

A further mass poisoning, this time of 6,000 people occurred in Manchester in 1900 when seventy people died from drinking local beer. Arsenic in the glucose used for brewing was present in levels that meant anyone drinking five pints of the brew would be ingesting a dangerously high dose and with many men drinking this amount of beer every working day the death toll is less than surprising.

Exposure to arsenical compounds in consumer goods such as fabric dyes and wallpapers was also commonplace, especially for those who manufactured these products, and in the polluted air. Arsenic was even used in medical preparations to treat everything from asthma and cancer to reduced libido and skin problems. Yet William Farr, the Statistic Head of the General Register Office was to comment in 1840 that 'it is generally asked for to kill 'rats', but it is questionable whether arsenic kills more rats than human beings.' In France, arsenic came to be called *poudre de succession,* 'inheritance powder' and with a cumulative effect acting particularly on the liver and kidneys, it could be administered in small doses over a span of time until a critical level was reached, meaning that the poisoner could be comfortably far away when death occurred.

In Mary's day, the relatively inexpensive arsenic was readily available in a white oxide powder form derived from the metallic ore, the fatal dose known to be an amount equivalent in size to a pea. Once administered, the poison induced symptoms of irritation and burning to the throat, faintness, nausea and vomiting mucus flecked with blood. Progressive abdominal pain, respiratory constriction and a white 'furry' covering to the tongue signalled that within the next 12–18 hours, severe diarrhoea and a weakened, irregular pulse would cause collapse and result in death, the victim conscious until the end. 'Enlightened' doctors, familiar with the cholera symptoms occasionally seen in Mary's day, attributed murder to disease.

Eventually, because of the number of murder cases involving the poison, the government was forced to introduce in 1851 the 'Arsenic Act' forbidding the sale of any arsenic compounds to a purchaser who was unknown to the supplying pharmacist. Poison bottles were given distinctive features; coloured glasses like cobalt blue, inky black, and dark green ensured they were easily recognizable, as well as having raised lettering or inlays of the words 'POISON' or 'DEATH' on the glass, especially useful if you were fumbling by candlelight. Patterns included latticework, deep grooves, geometric shapes, and most commonly, the skull and crossbones, which would have been particularly useful in instances where the consumer was illiterate. Would-be poisoners however were further thwarted by the introduction of a requirement that all manufacturers of arsenic powder mix one ounce of a colouring agent (indigo or soot were employed) to every pound of arsenic powder produced.

But all that lay in the future. Mary, and many of her contemporaries, could buy arsenic with relative ease. In light of Mary's vocation as a career-poisoner, contextualising her crimes, several cases of note, also hailing from Yorkshire, warrant examination here. Hannah Whitley used a pie as the delivery medium for a fatal dose of arsenic, with the poison concentrated in the crust. Hannah claimed she had been coerced into the act of poisoning by her employer, a local linen weaver named Horseman, who was involved in an on-going feud with the intended victim, Thomas Rhodes, who lived in Hampsthwaite near Harrogate. Her culinary efforts had the desired effect as her pastry made the entire family ill, and resulted in the death of five-year-old Joseph Rhodes.

In her defence, Hannah claimed that Horseman had forced her to put the poison into Rhodes's food, threatening to kill her if she refused, and that the rest of the Rhodes family were not the intended victims. Nonetheless, while Horseman faced no formal proceedings, it was Hannah who paid the penalty with her life. She was hanged at the York Tyburn on 3 August 1789.

Twenty-two-year-old William Smith employed an ingenious and indeed seasonal method of administering arsenic to poison not only his stepfather but his two half-siblings as well. William's mother had married a man named Thomas Harper who already had two children of his own, William and Anne. Faced with the ultimate division and diminution of his inheritance, Smith purchased two pennyworth of arsenic from the local apothecary, whose suspicions he failed to arouse as he also purchased some remedies for his horses at the same time. He allegedly had a problem with rats in his barn. Smith decided the perfect way to administer the poison would be to mix it with the ingredients of the Good Friday cake that was being prepared for the household. But unbeknownst to Smith, a maid-servant had seen him interfering with the flour.

The Harpers' neighbours had been invited for the Easter treat too, but clearly providence was on their side when they were unable to make dinner, and as it turned out only Tom Harper and his two children ended up eating any of the fatal cake. As soon as the poison began to take effect, Smith fled to Liverpool, leaving his victims to suffer in agony until father and both children died the following day. In spite of the motives that had driven Smith's actions, he found that once on the run he was unable to live with his conscience, and returning home he was immediately arrested and confessed all. At the assizes of 1753, Smith's own confession, along with the evidence of the apothecary who had sold him the poison and that of the maid-servant who saw him tamper with the cake's ingredients, ensured he was found guilty and sentenced to death. On Monday 15 August Smith was hanged at the York Tyburn and afterwards his body sent for dissection.

In an attempt to avert any thorough investigation of the three Kitchin deaths, Mary put it about that plague had been the cause of their demise. During the 1780s, extensive building of back-to-back housing in Quarry Hill led to frequent outbreaks of typhoid, typhus fever and other diseases, thanks to the overcrowded and unsanitary living conditions. Bubonic plague had made repeated appearances in Leeds through the centuries, and though the last severe outbreak had occurred as long ago as 1645, when the disease struck in Vicar Lane, it had spread so quickly through the town that between March and December of that year over 1,300 people died. The collective memory of the deaths of over one fifth of the estimated 6,000 strong population of Leeds in the mid-seventeenth century was still keen, and by her inference of plague, Mary thereby ensured that there would be no unwanted enquiries, as the lasting fear of infection meant that nobody in the neighbourhood would venture near the Kitchin home or shop premises, the doors of which were prudently closed and padlocked.

Mary's nerves must have been tested however by the visiting doctor who attended the last surviving Kitchin sister on her deathbed. He was of the strong opinion that the sickness and sudden death bore the hallmarks of poisoning, and on examining many of the vessels and cooking utensils in the house, his suspicions were clearly aroused as he asked whether any water for poisoning flies had been used; a reasonable supposition as at this time, manufacturers included arsenic in fly papers. A typical flypaper contained 150–400mg of soluble arsenic salts, and was consequently the source of a potentially lethal dose, provided that it could be administered without arousing suspicion. By soaking such a flypaper in water, a would-be poisoner could extract most of the soluble arsenites within a few hours, obtaining a tea-coloured solution which could then be disguised in a cup of strong tea or coffee, or a glass of brandy. However, the dilutions of arsenic obtained from fly papers were also innocently employed by some women to enhance their looks in a homemade face wash, as would be highlighted in the 1889 murder trial of Florence Maybrick, accused of poisoning her husband, who when she came to give evidence in her defence, claimed the arsenic she had extracted from fly papers was purely for cosmetic use.

This turn of events must have alarmed Mary as the attending doctor also wanted to 'open the body' to perform an autopsy on the last Kitchin sister to die. It would be wrong to assume that the standards of forensic investigations practised by the medical fraternity at this time were crude, or to suggest that the surgeons were not competent in their conduct of autopsies. In 1752, matters had been improved for the advancement of anatomical study in England with the passing of an Act that allowed judges to substitute dissection instead of a sentence of hanging in a metal cage at the gibbet after execution and as we shall see a circumstance that is most pertinent to the story of Mary Bateman. However, as no family member was left alive to give their consent to the procedure, the body was buried without any investigation and Mary thus avoided detection. The last of the Kitchins was laid to rest in the same grave as her sister and her mother, presumably in the seventeenth century Quaker burial ground attached to the Friends' Meeting House, known as Camp Hill Court, between Water Lane and Great Wilson Street.

Some time after the funeral, the creditors were called in to assess the estate of the Kitchin sisters. Though their draper's shop was known to be an entirely solvent business, it was found that both house and shop were all but empty of goods and chattels, and the account books were also missing. Clearly, Mary had used the convenient closure of both premises due to 'plague' as a cover under which to strip both house and shop behind closed doors, to the extent that, when all claims on the estate had been adjudicated, the meagre belongings left met only eightpence in the pound for each creditor's total claim.

Obviously Mary had hit her stride as a poisoner. Unencumbered by any moral restraint, in the guise of a caring nurse or a well-meaning practitioner, Mary was skilled at presenting a persona of benevolence, masking her true intention. Killing someone with poison, by its very nature, requires careful planning and subterfuge, so it comes as no surprise that poisoners tend to be cunning, sneaky, and creative, and reliant on verbal and emotional manipulation, all attributes which could be applied to Mary in spades. As far as her motives for murder were concerned, they may have been driven by greed and the very real need to conceal her guilt, common factors influencing many other murderers past and present. Not counting those of her victims who must have earlier succumbed to her various 'remedies' and abortifacients, in the past she had been forced to resort to repayment to avoid prosecution for theft and extortion. Mary now availed herself of the advantage of using poison to silence her victims. And as long as she evaded detection, the feelings of power and control she experienced as a result of her successes over those whose expectations she had raised, and upon those whose fears she had played (while all the time draining their purses) must had increased her confidence in her future endeavours. Even so, following the deaths of the Kitchin family, presumably as a precautionary measure, Mary must have persuaded her husband that it would be prudent to quit March Lane; it was time to move again, and for Mary to manufacture her most audacious and public exploit yet, and one of a sacrilegious nature.

Chapter 4

'Crist is coming'

The extent of John Bateman's awareness of, or complicity in his wife's criminality at this point can only be guessed at. They removed as a couple to new lodgings in Black Dog Yard; another shrewd and necessary relocation in view of Mary's increasing notoriety. Black Dog Yard was within an area of Leeds known as 'Bank', the Black Dog Inn close to the junction with East Street and Cross Green Lane. Bank was the focus for those property developers, mentioned in the first chapter, who capitalised on the cheap land upon which to build the haphazard development of back-to-back housing, which they rented out to the poor workers, invariably employed in the numerous mills proliferating in Leeds at the time. While some of the terraces were never finished, the building of others was begun in open fields. As the tenements of slum dwellings grew, access was gained by a narrow tunnel reaching the back halves of the houses off narrow unmetalled roads, thus saving ground so that even more houses could be crammed onto a site; after all, access roads and pavements were wasted space which brought in no rent to the landlord.

Inside, the houses were cramped, with two rooms, one up, one down, about fourteen feet square, often with a cellar, presenting an additional rental income when let out as a one-room dwelling. The precise conditions in these hovels were not officially catalogued until the 1830s, when the Whig government of that decade appointed Edwin Chadwick to carry out his investigation into the working classes. So, although the details that follow postdate the Batemans' period, they nevertheless reflect conditions in the opening years of the century.

One seventeen-year-old flax mill worker named Eliza Marshall told a government inspector in 1832, 'I live in a cellar. I pay 1s a week for it. I have no mother. I live with my little sisters.' Eliza had worked in the factories from the age of nine, and by the time she was eleven she was starting to go lame due to the long hours and harsh conditions. By the age of seventeen, she was too ill to work. As there was no piped water supply or proper sewerage system, the 'necessary' (lavatory) was often a wooden screen round a hole dug in the ground. Sometimes there weren't even any 'out offices,' or outside toilets, so people used a bucket which would be emptied onto a common midden heap. In 1832, during the first and one of the worst cholera epidemics to hit Leeds, seventy-five cartloads of soil were removed from just one of the privies in Boot & Shoe Yard in Kirkgate. Over a decade later things had not improved, as a report on the Sanitary Conditions in Leeds published in 1845 stated that:

> 'By far the most unhealthy localities of Leeds are close squares of houses, or yards, as they are called, which have been erected for the accommodation of working people. Some of these, though situated in comparatively high ground, are airless from the enclosed structure, and being wholly unprovided with any form of under-drainage or convenience, or arrangements for cleansing, are one mass of damp and filth … The ashes, garbage and filth of all kinds are thrown from the doors and windows of the houses upon the surface of the streets and courts … The privies are few in proportion to the inhabitants. They are open to view both in front and rear, are invariably in a filthy condition, and often remain without removal of the filth for six months.'

However insalubrious the Batemans' new surrounding were (the conditions of 'filth' alluded to above were yet to reach their zenith) the fact remained that they were a safe mile or so from Marsh Lane. They were also a decent remove from the Anchor Inn in Kirkgate where the proprietor, a Mr Crookes, had recently outwitted Mary's attempted theft of a watch. She had had more success, however, in stealing some linen laid out to dry on a hedge. Hedges and bushes were often used to dry washing outdoors in the summertime, in the fresh air while the sun bleached it, especially where there were no open fields to use as tenter-grounds for the same purpose. This bold theft was from under the nose of the lad who'd been set to watch over it; no doubt he received a serious scolding later for his inattentiveness.

Doubtless Mary continued with her deceitful ways, keeping up her thefts and malign ministrations to the susceptible needy. However, it was while the Batemans were living in Black Dog Yard that Mary conceived of her most masterly and far reaching scam to date, with a cash incentive to exploit the variations to orthodox Christian beliefs which flourished toward the close of the eighteenth century. As religious tolerance gained in strength, the growing zeal arising from the beliefs in the ministries of the self-proclaimed prophetess Joanna Southcott increased in popularity. Her following flourished in the climate of expectant frenzy whipped up by her and the assertions of other visionaries that the return of Jesus Christ was imminent. Another zealot emerging in the arena of religious radicalism was Richard Brothers, who, in 1793, declared himself to be the apostle of a new religion, proclaiming himself to be Prince of the Hebrews, a literal descendant of the Biblical House of David, and the Nephew of the Almighty, who decreed he was to rule over Israel until the return of Jesus Christ.

To put into context the implausibility of belief in the unbelievable exploit which Mary put into practice, both Southcott and Brothers, whose careers overlapped, had attracted quite a following, in spite of their apparently far-fetched assertions. Joanna's devotees, referred to as 'Southcottians', were said to have numbered over 100,000. Around the year 1792, Southcott had become persuaded that she possessed supernatural gifts. She wrote and dictated prophecies in rhyme, and then identified herself as the woman spoken of in the Book of Revelation who would give birth to the new Messiah. Incredibly, at the age of sixty-four, the virgin Southcott announced that she was indeed pregnant and would in due course be delivered of the messianic 'man child', the Shiloh of Genesis. The date of 19 October 1814 was that fixed for the birth, but Shiloh failed to appear. It was given out that Southcott was in a trance. She died not long afterwards at the end of December, her followers refusing to release her body for some time as they believed she would rise from the dead. They agreed to her burial only after the corpse began to decay.

Richard Brothers based his declarations on the premise that he had a special divine commission. Claiming to hear the voice of an attending angel, who proclaimed to him the fall of Babylon the Great, which, according to Brothers, was in fact London, his plea for mercy was apparently heard by God and London was spared. Brothers was also anticipating the arrival of a heavenly lady who, descending from the clouds, would shower him with money, love and happiness. In February 1792, declaring himself a healer with the ability to restore sight to the blind, he drew large crowds, not so much in demand for his alleged healing ability, as for the small gifts of money he paid out to those he prayed for. Ordained with the special role of gathering and returning the Jews to Palestine, in particular the 'Jews' who were hidden amongst the population of Britain, Brothers maintained he would achieve this by using a rod he had made from a wild rosebush, with which he would perform miracles, much as Moses had done with his staff, to produce water from a rock and to part the Red Sea. Later on, in consequence of his prophesying the death of King George III and an end to the monarchy of Great Britain, Brothers was arrested for treason in 1795, and imprisoned on the grounds of being criminally insane.

From a private asylum in Islington, Brothers predicted that on 19 November 1795 he would be revealed as Prince of the Hebrews and Ruler of the world. However, when the date came and passed without any such manifestation, his disillusioned followers drifted away, many swelling the ranks of the Southcottians. Brothers spent the last 30 years of his life designing flags and uniforms and drew up plans for a palace in the New Jerusalem. His release from the asylum was finally secured in 1806, the same year in which Mary Bateman's hen laid its first miraculous egg.

Like many other housewives of her time, Mary kept several hens to keep her supplied with fresh eggs. As her reputation as a fortune teller had begun to suffer as a consequence of the increasing complaints inevitable from her deceived clientele, Mary changed tack, and jumping on the spiritual bandwagon, announced that she had been granted a vision in which she had been told that one of her hens would lay fourteen special eggs and that the last one would mark the beginning of the Apocalypse. By this time, thanks to the impact of Brothers and Southcott, the popularity of Millenarianism was assured and had gained a remarkable hold on the collective imagination. Right on cue then, one of Mary's hens laid an egg with the inscription 'Crist is coming' written on the shell.

Mary was astute enough to embellish the miracle, and shore-up her shaky reputation, by claiming that she herself was a devotee of Joanna Southcott, who in 1802 had begun 'sealing' her followers by giving them a special token to mark them out as being among the 144,000 to be 'saved' according to the Book of Revelation. These were the survivors of the Twelve Tribes of Israel, sealed as servants of God on their foreheads. Mary had somehow managed to secure one of these genuine tokens and, while one should not jump to conclusions, presumably by nefarious means. Her status as one of Southcott's 'sealed' reinforced her announcement that not only did the eggs laid by her hen proclaim Christ's second coming, but that they foretold it would happen *very soon*. Cashing in on the mounting hysteria caused by this pronouncement of the imminence of Doomsday, Mary put the prophetic hen on display, charging the faithful between a penny and a shilling a look. Mary also began selling to believers her own version of Southcott's 'proclamations of faith', special 'seals' (a piece of paper bearing the initials 'JC') which she assured would guarantee the bearer admission into Heaven following the Apocalypse. Thousands of visitors came to be saved, and at the same time lined Mary's pockets.

In relatively recent memory, several 'portents' had occurred. In the autumn of 1799, the sky had been ablaze with strange electrical storms and lights. On 19 November, over Huncoates, in Lincolnshire, a ball of fire was seen to blaze across the heavens, leaving a trail of flashes behind it, while seven days prior to this celestial spectacle, in the skies above Hereford the moon was seen to shine with a fierce glow and a 'large red pillar of fire', preceded to the south by 'flashes of extremely vivid electrical sort'. This display, accompanied by short dazzling flashes and pulses, coalescing together, then suddenly bursting apart, shooting trails of fire across the night sky was witnessed by many, the meteorological fireworks display taken by most, with typical end-of-the-century-foreboding, as a clear apocalyptic omen.

It is difficult to say how long Mary's holy hoax would have continued, and how much more money she would have made, had not a sceptical doctor managed one morning to examine one of the 'freshly laid' miraculous eggs. He got up early, hid near her house and found that the inscription had been written in a corrosive concentrated vinegar, Mary re-applying the message until it was partially burned into the shell of the egg. The misspelling of 'Crist' was also a giveaway, although by contemporary standards Mary had what was then considered a reasonable education for the daughter of an agricultural labourer, possibly attained at Sunday School, where she had learned to read and write; accomplishments she was later to use remorselessly against her more gullible 'clients'. When the authorities were made aware of the deception, Black Dog Yard was raided and Mary was actually caught in the cruel act of re-inserting an inscribed egg back into the chicken's egg duct, ready to be 'laid' again later. The ruse exposed, the resulting scandal forced Joanna Southcott to stop 'sealing' her own followers because of the stigma of Mary's fraud. As for the celebrated chicken, Mary profited a final few pennies from the bird by selling it to a still curious neighbour, who on finding that none of the subsequent eggs that it laid bore any mystic messages, wrung its neck and put it in the pot. The records are ominously silent on the 'authorities' who would eventually stop Mary in her tracks. There was no Yorkshire Constabulary in the modern sense of the term until the 1830s when boroughs were given the right to establish police forces along Metropolitan (London) lines in their own areas. The men who raided Black Dog Yard were almost certainly Constables of the Watch under the direction of a magistrate.

Oddly enough, after toying with people's religious devotions for the better part of a month, rather than for the monstrous hoax she'd played out, Mary was most resented for her cruelty to chickens. And it is the image of Mary holding up the 'miracle egg' which graced the frontispiece of the book detailing her exploits, trial and execution, which would run to a twelfth edition two years after its first publication in 1811, two years after she was hanged.

This engraving of Mary was a somewhat emblematic representation of 'The Yorkshire Witch'. Along with the infamous egg, on the writing desk at which Mary is sitting is another item with religious overtones – a bottle bearing on the label the words 'M. Bateman's Balm of Gilead'. Balm of Gilead is a high-quality ointment with healing properties extracted from resin taken from a flowering plant in the Middle East. The Bible uses the term 'balm of Gilead' metaphorically as an example of something with healing or soothing powers; clearly this is the illustrator's jibe at the supposed curative preparations that were later to become Mary's hallmark. The further poignant inclusion in the engraving is that of pens and ink on the desk, and a letter addressed to William Perigo, whose significance will become apparent in due course.

Mary's exploitation of the Southcott phenomenon was not however restricted to her prophetic chickens. Perhaps in a bid to avoid the local fallout from her apocalyptic predictions, and capitalising on the susceptible nature of unquestioning Southcottians, Mary contrived to combine a convenient removal from Leeds with another fraudulent undertaking and took a trip to York. Enough time had passed since her last hasty departure from that city, when she had fled to Leeds in 1788 after the thefts from her then mistress had come to light. On her arrival in the city, Mary astutely sought out and attended meetings of York's Southcott followers. The License Register kept by the ecclesiastic authorities recording all Protestant dissenters' meetings confirms a proliferation of such gatherings in the city, with licenses granted for worship in private houses before a national network of Southcottian chapels was established after 1811. Posing as a devoted follower of Southcott, we can imagine Mary, the consummate actress, joining in with the proceedings, which included the distribution of 'wine and cakes', hymn singing, the reading of Southcott's prophecies and 'the lifting up of hands for Christ's Kingdom to come'. And from one of those York congregations Mary selected for herself a likely and receptive victim, settling on a poor widow living in alms housing who she identified as being ripe for exploitation.

After following the widow home to find out where she lived, Mary knocked on her door, seemingly at random, and explained that she was a stranger who had come to York for a few days, and was seeking the company of fellow Southcottians. When the widow told her that there were many followers in the city, and indeed she herself was one, Mary congratulated herself on her good fortune in happening upon a fellow believer. She next enquired whether there were any Southcottians in the city who might be able to accommodate her during her stay as it was her 'particular wish to be in kindred company'. When the widow could think of nobody in a position to offer her lodgings, on seeing Mary's exaggerated and feigned disappointment, the widow had the charity to offer Mary to share her own bed – even though it would be an inconvenience; Mary did seem after all to be 'a clean kind of woman'. In the eighteenth century it was not unusual for people, even relative strangers, of the same sex to share a bed – difficulties of transport often made overnight stays a necessity and the sharing of rooms and beds was tolerated, particularly in houses where space was restricted.

Once through the door, next on Mary's agenda was the reconnoitring of the widow's dwelling, to mentally mark down whatever possessions might be worth stealing. To make a thorough survey however she would need the widow out of the way. Mary suggested with another lie, that as she was not at all acquainted with the streets of York herself, perhaps the widow would be kind enough to purchase on her behalf a little meat. However, the widow was wary at leaving a person of such recent acquaintance alone in her home so a girl was sent on the errand instead. On her return with some mutton, once boiled, Mary gobbled down the lot, offering only the broth to her hostess, whose refusal to partake of even a spoonful seemed to unduly enrage Mary. In spite of her insistent urgings, the broth was eventually thrown out, and as Mary herself had refused to touch the proffered dish, in all probability the widow had avoided being poisoned by her house guest, whose likely intention was to steal the old lady's belongings unimpeded.

Chapter 1

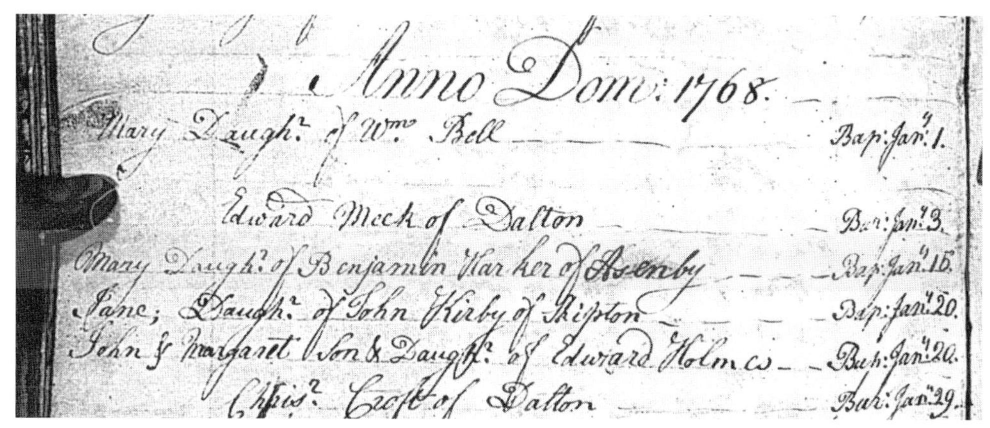

Anno Dom: 1768.

Mary Daugh.r of Wm Bell — Bap: Jan.y 1.

Edward Meek of Dalton — Bap: Jan.y 3.

Mary Daugh.r of Benjamin Harker of Asenby — Bap: Jan.y 15.

Jane; Daugh.r of John Kirby of Skipton — Bap: Jan.y 20.

John & Margaret Son & Daught.r of Edward Holmes — Bap: Jan.y 20.

Chris.r Croft of Dalton — Bap: Jan.y 29.

Excerpt from the 1768 Baptismal records for St Columba's Church, Topcliffe. The baptism of Mary Harker on 15 January is the third entry for that year. (*Courtesy of The North Yorkshire County Records Office*)

Topcliffe and the church of St Columba, seen from Asenby – the village of Mary's birth.

Old Market Cross, Topcliffe. The remains of the old Market Cross and the cobble surround hark back to Topcliffe's former prominence in staging one of the largest annual fairs in the north of England. Since 1327, Topley Fair as the event was affectionately known, was a traditional rendezvous for gypsies and horse-dealers from far and wide, and a raucous three-day event that would have been familiar to Mary, the fair probably the colourful highpoint of her calendar.

While Leeds, by the standards of the time, was a large town when Mary relocated there from York in 1788, these two views show something of a still-pastoral landscape giving way to the growing industrialisation of the early nineteenth century. Above, 'Leeds from the Meadows' by Joseph Rhodes (courtesy of the Leeds City Art Gallery) and below, Turner's somewhat romanticised view of Leeds at a time when industry had not yet fully taken a grip on what was previously no more than a rural town.

The Old Parish Church of St Peter as it would have appeared at the time of Mary Harker's marriage to John Bateman – the old church was pulled down in 1838 to make way for the present parish church, re-opened in September 1841. Robinson's Relics of Old Leeds (1896). (*Image courtesy of The Victorian Web*)

Old Buildings in Yard off Briggate, Leeds. In view of the exposure of some of Mary's early frauds and thefts, a little over a year after their marriage, the Batemans prudently moved from High Court Lane and took a house in Mr Wells' yard, a spirit merchant who lived on Briggate. While the accommodation in High Court Lane had been furnished, the couple apparently furnished their new abode in Wells' Yard themselves in "a tolerable comfortable manner", possibly financed by Mary's various thefts and scams, many of which must have escaped notice. Robinson's Relics of Old Leeds (1896). (*Image courtesy of The Victorian Web*)

Chapter 2

The Moot Hall, Briggate, Leeds
Situated at the Kirkgate junction with Commercial Street, absent from this drawing are the stocks and pillory once occupying the area in front of the Hall. Though the original seventeenth century building was replaced by one erected in 1710, it was still considered a hindrance to traffic, the narrowness of the roadways on either side of the Hall making it difficult for two carriages to pass one another; consequently, in 1822 the decision was made to demolish it. Robinson's depiction shows the Moot Hall, built in 1710 that would have been familiar to Mary, replete with the statue of Queen Anne. Robinson's Relics of Old Leeds (1896). (*Image courtesy of The Victorian Web*)

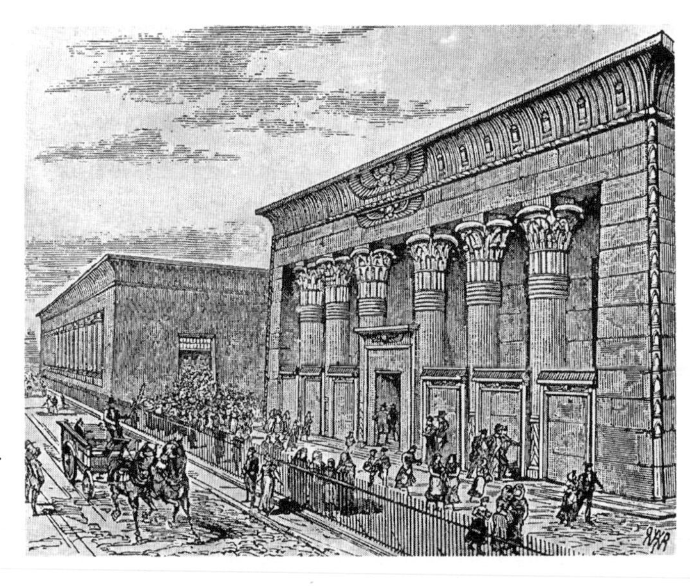

Exterior view of Marshall's Flax Mill, situated on Water Lane in the industrial district of Holbeck on the western outskirts of Leeds. After the serious fire which broke out on 13 February 1796, countless mill workers were injured and at least ten others perished in the blaze when one of the mill walls collapsed. Mary Bateman saw a financial opportunity to make good on the tragedy however.

'A Day at a Leeds Flax Mill' Drawing of Marshall's Mills, Holbeck showing the operators at their machines. During the eighteenth century fires like the one which devastated Marshall's were commonplace in mills, with the processing of flax creating a highly combustible dust, and the risk exacerbated by hot machine bearings lubricated with linseed oil, as well as the additional risk posed by workers using candles to light the mill.

Supplementary Militia, turning out for Twenty Days Amusement. —'The French Invade us hay!'—damme whose afraid!

Caricaturist James Gillray's satirical view of the Supplementary Militia, published in 1796, the year that John Bateman joined the ranks.

Mentha pulegium – Pennyroyal (Botanical illustration from William Woodville's 'Medical Botany' published in 1793). As well as telling fortunes, Mary developed a lucrative sideline offering her services as an abortionist. Pennyroyal was a well-known herbal abortifacient, the ingestion of which however can also result in irreversible renal damage, severe liver damage and death.

Chapter 3

Gipton Spa Bath House

The Misses Kitchin, two Quaker sisters who were the first identifiable victims of Mary as a career-poisoner, ran a draper's shop in St Peter's Square, in Georgian times falling within the fashionable and genteel spa area of Leeds where people came to take the beneficial waters. A vestige of Leeds as a spa resort, the open air Gipton Spa Bath House still stands intact in Gledhow Valley Woods, on the Gledhow Valley Road near its junction with Roundhay Road; the waters were celebrated in the district, the great Leeds antiquarian, Ralph Thoresby (1658-1725) being a frequent visitor.

Further precautions were introduced in the mid-1800s in a bid to prevent accidental arsenic poisonings: the distinctive blue glass of this arsenic bottle was one such measure, making it easily recognisable, even if the label were missing, along with the raised ridged glass (especially useful if you were fumbling by candlelight). Would-be poisoners however were further thwarted by the introduction of a requirement that all manufacturers of arsenic powder mix one ounce of a colouring agent (indigo or soot were employed) to every pound of arsenic powder produced, and while these measures may have arrested the trend in the use of this particular poison, it was cold comfort for those of Mary's victims who had already succumbed. (*Image courtesy of the Wellcome Trust*)

THE GREAT LOZENGE-MAKER.

A Hint to Paterfamilias.

The Great Lozenge-Maker. A Hint to Paterfamilias by caricaturist John Leech
This cartoon, first published in Punch in November 1858, alludes to the high-profile 'Bradford Humbug Poisoning', an incident involving the accidental arsenic poisoning of more than 200 people. The symptoms of Mary's victims were indicative of her employing arsenic which, as a by-product of the emerging smelting industry, was inexpensive and readily available from pharmacists and apothecary shops and popular as a rat killer. Though accidental ingestion accounted for many deaths by arsenic poisoning, as attested to by the incident in Bradford, because of the level of murders cases in nineteenth century England involving the poison, the government were forced to introduce in 1851 the 'Arsenic Act' forbidding the sale of any arsenic compounds to a purchaser who was unknown to the supplying pharmacist.

Chapter 4

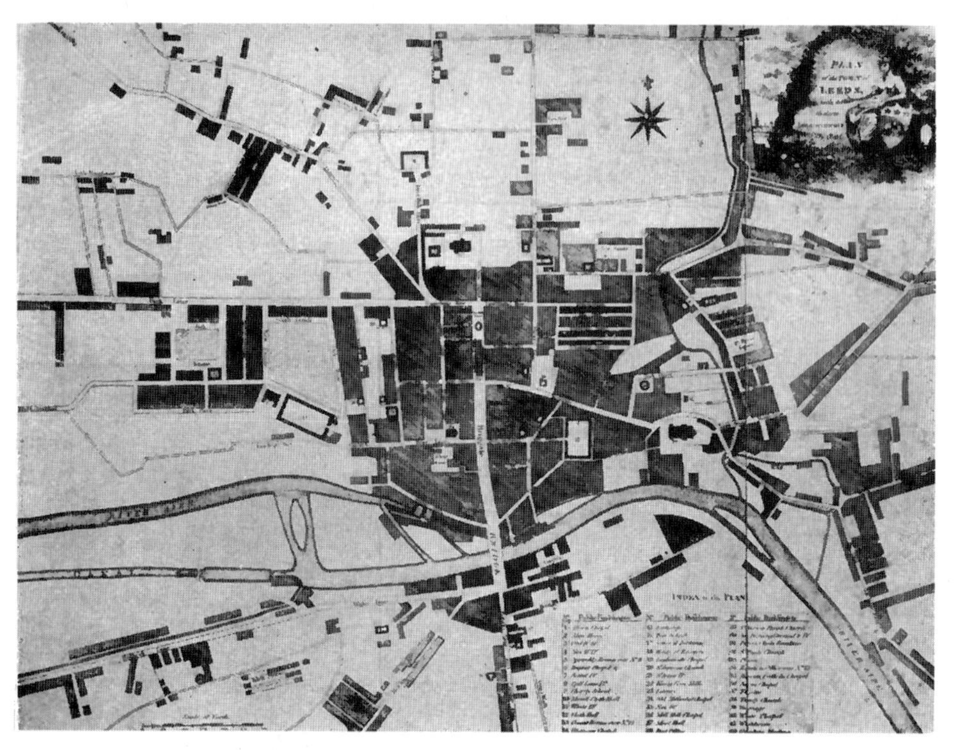

Map of Leeds dating from 1806 showing the spread of urban development. By this date the Batemans had moved again, to Black Dog Yard, within an area of Leeds known as 'Bank' which fell within the area of spreading housing seen in the southeast corner of the map.

Self-proclaimed prophetess Joanna Southcott
Claiming herself to be a devotee of Joanna Southcott, whose following of 'Southcottians' flourished in the climate of expectant frenzy whipped up by her assertions that the return of Jesus Christ was imminent, Mary was able shore-up her shaky reputation prior to announcing that she had been granted a vision in which she had been told that one of her hens would lay fourteen miraculous eggs, the last of which would signal the beginning of the Apocalypse.

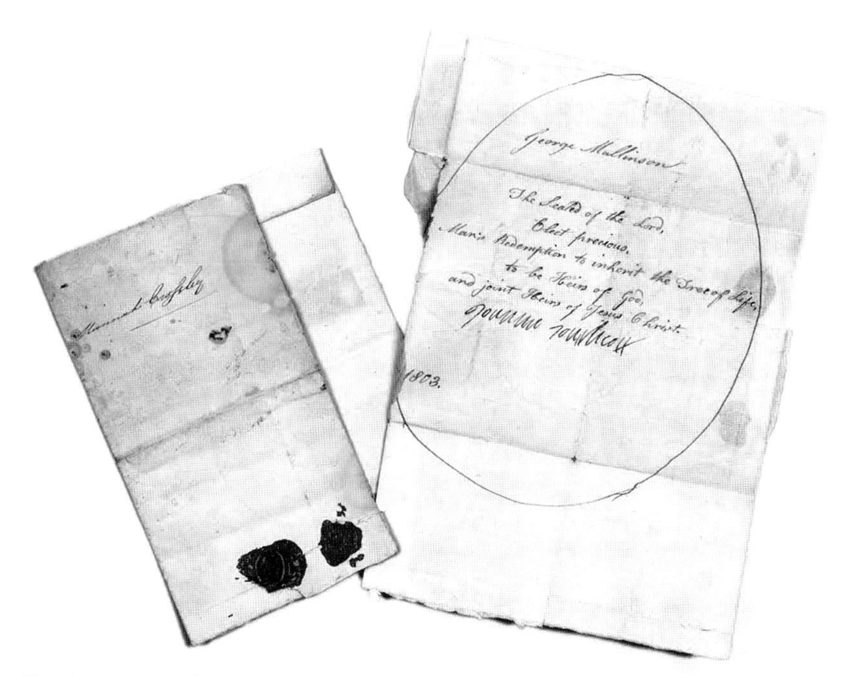

Joanna Southcott was able to count how many followers she had by the number of people she had 'sealed'. Lord Byron described these proclamations as considered by many to be 'Passports to Heaven'. Within an inscribed oval, each 'seal' had the same wording inside and was signed by Joanna Southcott, and her own seal affixed, confirming that the 'sealed' person had renounced Satan. Southcott claimed not to charge for these passports coveted by her followers, however Mary did charge and profit from the sale of her own versions of Southcott's 'proclamations of faith'. (*Image courtesy of Bonhams of London*)

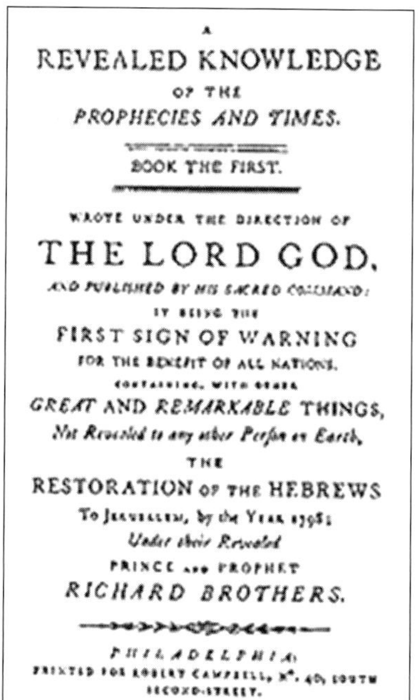

A
REVEALED KNOWLEDGE
OF THE
PROPHECIES AND TIMES.

BOOK THE FIRST.

WROTE UNDER THE DIRECTION OF
THE LORD GOD,
AND PUBLISHED BY HIS SACRED COMMAND:
IT BEING THE
FIRST SIGN OF WARNING
FOR THE BENEFIT OF ALL NATIONS.
CONTAINING, WITH OTHER
GREAT AND *REMARKABLE* THINGS,
Not Revealed to any other Person on Earth,
THE
RESTORATION OF THE HEBREWS
To Jerusalem, by the Year 1798;
Under their Revealed
PRINCE AND PROPHET
RICHARD BROTHERS.

PHILADELPHIA:
PRINTED FOR ROBERT CAMPBELL, No. 40, SOUTH
SECOND-STREET.
1795.

Title page of *A Revealed Knowledge of the Prophecies and Times* written by Richard Brothers in 1795, the year he was committed to a lunatic asylum. Brothers was a contemporary of Joanna Southcott, their careers overlapping; he was another zealot emerging in the climate of religious radicalism which facilitated Mary's audacious and sacrilegious hoax.

Detail from the frontispiece of *The Extraordinary Life and Character of Mary Bateman* (abbreviated title) published in 1811. In her right hand Mary holds up the infamous hen's egg bearing the inscription 'Crist is coming'.

Old Leeds Bridge

It was on the old Leeds Bridge that Mary, in one of her more petty enterprises of theft, posed as a cook in order to intercepted a hapless butcher's delivery boy; relieving him of another customer's purchase; scolding him she gave the lad a thump on the back for good measure.

Chapter 5

In telling fortunes and providing 'Love charms' and magical cures, Mary employed the alter-ego of a 'Mrs Moore', later supplanted by the equally fictitious 'Miss Blythe'. Both of these spurious seers were equally adept at seeing into the future though the latter was an exponent in the removal of "evil wishes", their clients charged exorbitantly through the agency of Mary. This design for a love amulet comes from the eighteenth century *Black Pullet Grimoire*; the book also contained instruction on how to produce the 'Black Pullet' (from which the book takes its title) otherwise known as the 'Hen that lays Golden Eggs' – not such a far remove perhaps from Mary Bateman's money-making 'miraculous' egg laying hen.

Chapter 7

The Female Prison, York

The 'Female Prison' was built in 1780, adjacent to the Debtor's Prison, in a bid to ease that gaol's overcrowding. At the end of the seventeenth century, it was decided to build a new prison inside the bailey of York Castle and work commenced on the new County Gaol which opened in 1705, having taken four years to build – this building became known as the Debtor's prison but proved inadequate with regards to the increasing prisoner population.

Chapter 8

York's County Courthouse
The impressive façade of the Female Prison mirrored the architecture of the newly appointed County Court situated opposite, designed by John Carr and completed three years earlier in 1777. Here Mary Bateman was tried for the wilful murder of Rebecca Perigo on Friday 17 March 1809.

Judge Simon Le Blanc (c.1748–1816)
Depicted by portraitist John Opie as a country gentleman, Le Blanc would have been attired in the traditional scarlet robes lined with ermine and wearing a full-bottomed wig in the seventeenth century style when he presided over Mary's trial during the Lent Assizes of 1809.

Thomas Rowlandson's depiction of a court hearing at the Old Bailey, drawn in the same year that Mary Bateman was tried, gives an idea of the judicial proceedings that would have taken place.

Hogarth's 'The Reward of Cruelty'
The body of a convicted and executed criminal has been delivered to the Royal College of Surgeons for an anatomy lesson. This was the fate that also befell Mary's corpse, a stipulation of her sentence in accordance with the 'Murder Act' passed in 1752, mandating the dissection of the bodies of executed murderers.

Rowlandson's 'A Gibbet' (c. 1790's) – two riders start back in horror before the ghastly corpse dangling in its iron cage. A prolific caricaturist, Rowlandson (1756–1827) seemed to have a fascination with death, scaffolds and gibbets; though the 'Murder Act' sanctioned the dissection of both sexes, 'gibbeting' was reserved for male malefactors found guilty of particularly heinous or high profile crimes. (*Courtesy of York Art Gallery, York Museums Trust*)

Chapter 9

Rowlandson's artistic predilections are further evidenced by his 'Execution Day at York'. (*Courtesy of York Art Gallery, York Museums Trust*)

The interior of the condemned cell, York Castle Gaol (*Courtesy of York Museums Trust*)

D9913/3

The Last Dying Words, Speech, and Confession of JOSEPH BROWN and MARY BATEMAN, who were executed at the Drop behind the Castle of York, on Monday the 20th of March, 1809, BROWN for the wilful Murder of Mrs. Elizabeth Fletcher—and BATEMAN for the wilful Murder of Rebecca Perrigo.

The following is the voluntary Confession of that wicked and abandoned Wretch

JOSEPH BROWN, late of Cawood. He said he was 34 years of age, was born at Cotterelwood, in the West-Riding, by trade a flaxdresser, that he had been acquainted with Joseph Hazlegrove from his youth, and for the last six years, had been his constant companion and associate. In October 1804, they lodged at the house of Mrs. Elizabeth Fletcher, of Henley, near Ferrybridge; that he bought of Mr. Parker, an apothecary of Snaith, one ounce of laudanum, and on the 22d of the same month, about 9 o'clock at night, at supper, he and Hazlegrove gave to Mrs. Fletcher the laudanum in some warm ale sweetened with sugar, by which means she died; presently after they both went to bed, got up again in the night, and took from Mrs. Fletcher's pocket the key of her box; Hazlegrove opened the box, and took thereout a guinea and a half, after which they went away for Cawood, and were taken up and examined by the Magistrates, but for want of evidence were set at liberty. In January 1805, he received a quantity of linen cloaths and some black silk from Joseph Hazlegrove, which had been stolen from Mrs. Clarke, of Cawood: That on the 5th of November, 1805, he and Hazlegrave, about 8 o'clock at night, robbed and murdered Geo. Calvert, on the King's highway, between Fenton and Peckfield, for which crime they were both committed to York Castle, and at the Lent Assizes, 1806, were tried, but for want of sufficient evidence were acquitted. At the Summer Assizes following they were indicted for stealing three hams, a flitch and a half of bacon, a flitch of beef, a pig's cheek, and two sacks from Mr. John Boulton, of Barkin, for which crime they received sentence of death, but reprieved for transportation, and afterwards permitted to enlist into his Majesty's Royal York Rangers. He further confessed, that he and Hazlegrove had committed divers other felonies, robberies, and misdemeanors in the County of York, &c. By virtue of the above confession, they were both committed to the Castle of York, on the 11th day of February last, but no Bill was found against Hazlegrove, consequently he well be sent to his Regiment, the Royal York Rangers.

MARY BATEMAN, aged 41, who now forfeits her life for *Witchcraft and Murder*, practised with every agravation that extortion, protracted, and painful death could invent; accompanied by the most unprecedented instances of credulity that ever engaged public attention.

It appeared that in August, 1806, an application was made to this woman by Perrigo to cure his wife of a nervous complaint. Mary, with becoming *modesty*, declined to undertake the cure herself, but said that she had a Friend at Scarborough, a Miss Blyth, who could "read the stars," and collect from them the knowledge requisite to remove all corporeal and mental maladies, and as a preliminary step, required that Perrigo's wife should send her flannel petticoat to Miss Blyth, in order that she might from that article of dress, collect a knowledge of her disorder: Soon after Perrigo went to consult Mary Bateman, and while by her arts she was fleecing him of all the money he had or could possibly raise, amounting to Forty Guineas, the imaginary Miss Blyth ordered diffrent sums of money to be paid to Mary Bateman, to be inclosed in small bags, into which if either his own curiosity, or the still stronger curiosity of his wife, should induce them to look, the charm would be broken, and sudden death would be the consequence. Similar requests were repeated and complied with, under a promise, however, that they should at the expiration of eighteen months be allowed to open the bags, and these bags, they were told, would be found to contain all the money they had advanced. Mary requested to have a *live goose*, in order that it might be offered as a burnt-offering to her Familiar, and thereby destroy the works of darkness; she next demanded a counterpain and sheets; 4lb of bacon; next a cheese; then a pair of lamb's wool stockings; exclusive of money, bed, china, gowns, petticoats and family bible. In May, 1807 this prophet of ill predicted that both Perrigo and his wife would during the month, take a very severe illness; but they where consoled by the assurance that if they followed her prescriptions stedfastly, this illness would not be unto death. Mary Bateman received, as she said, a packet from Scarbrough; this packet contained a powerful charm, which was to be mixed up in a pudding, to be prepared for the purpose, and of which Perrigo and his wife were to eat, but on no account to allow any person to partake with them; and if it made them sick, as it probably would, they were to take each a spoonful of honey, mixed up with certain ingredients and if they took it all, without being deterred by the apparent illness it might produce, Mary assured them, *that their sorrow would be at an end!* Her words were too true, Perrigo's wife adhered stedfastly to the prescriptions, and her life paid the forfeit of her folly. The husband, less faithful, escaped with his life, and nothing more. Part of the Pudding was, by way of experiment, given to a cat, and it died; some fowls also picked up other parts of it, and shared the same fate.

How deeply infatuated the ill fated wife of Perrigo was, may be collected from the following fact;—On the Friday previous to the Sunday on which she died, while writhing under the most excruciating torture from the effects of the deleterious drugs prescribed by Mary Bateman, in the name of Miss Blyth, she extorted from her husband a promise, that even if her illness should issue in her death, a circumstance she did not much expect, he would continue to follow the directions of the sorceress, till the arrival of the time when all their expectations of freedom from the powers of darkness should be consummated in a happy fruition. In an evil hour he gave the promise, and scrupulously adhered to it till forced, by hard necessity, to violate an engagement more honourable in the breach than in the observance. The wife died on the 16th of May, 1807, in the greatest agonies and a letter arrived two or three days after from Miss Blyth, in which she attributed her death to having ventured to touch the enchanted bags.—Nor was the effects of this disobedience to end here; "inasmuch," said this disciple of the black art, in a letter to Perrigo, "as your wife has done this wicked "thing, she shall rise from the grave—stroke your face "with the cold hand of death—and you shall lose the use "of one side." In this way she continued to practice upon his hopes and fears; but terror being the more powerful engine upon minds so constituted as his, it was most frequently resorted to, and, unhappily, with too much success. Driven by his wants to brave all dangers, and to open the mysterious bags, where all his wealth was, as he imagined, deposited, but what must have been his surprise and vexation, to find that the contents of these bags were not worth one penny! He hurried to the sorceress, upbraided her with the wicked fraud, and told her that those bags contained nothing of value—"Aye," said Mary, "this comes of being in too great a hurry; you have opened them too soon." "Too soon, did you say," cried Perrigo, indignantly, who had now opened his eyes to his folly, "I think I have opened them too late." The bubble now burst; he laid his hopeless case before some of his neighbours; by their direction she was apprehended; when brought before the Magistrates she confessed there was no such person as Miss Blyth, but that the whole was a mere phantom, conjured up to forward her vile purposes.

W. Storry, Printer, York.

An original copy of the Broadsheet sold on the day of Mary's execution, detailing 'The last dying words, speech and confession of Joseph Brown and Mary Bateman…' Brown had also been found guilty of murder by poisoning at the Lent Assizes and was hanged alongside Mary. (*Courtesy of York Museums Trust*)

Chapter 10

Sarah Malcolm, convicted triple murderess, painted by William Hogarth in the condemned cell of Newgate Gaol two days before her execution on Wednesday 7 March 1733. Her notoriety was such that prints of the portrait were sold for sixpence each to a morbidly curious public – Hogarth is reputed to have said of his subject 'I see by this woman's features, that she is capable of any wickedness.' While no profit was made from the reproduction of an image of Mary, the treatment of her corpse post-mortem certainly presented a lucrative financial opportunity to monopolise on the notoriety of her name.

The only near contemporaneous image of Mary is the engraving for the frontispiece of *The Extraordinary Life and Character of Mary Bateman* published in 1811, two years after her execution.

Mary only stayed a couple of nights with the widow, but predictably after her departure it was discovered that she had made off with not only the few guineas in the widow's possession, but also some items of clothing. Needless to say, the widow never laid eyes on Mary again.

On her return to Leeds following her profitable stay in York, with the memory of the holy hen still fresh in people's minds and having thoroughly worked the Bank quarter of the town, Mary and John again moved, this time to lodgings near the Old Assembly Rooms in Kirkgate. Switching her energies and focus back to medicinal remedies and her side-line as an abortionist, in spite of those clients whose health began to falter after seeking Mary's assistance, her customer base nonetheless remained healthy, even if those who took her potions didn't, and her services were again in high demand.

Her thieving and prophesying weren't entirely side-lined however. Shortly after the miracle egg debacle, Mary, while benevolently nursing a neighbour, Rebecca Fisher, the expectant mother of seven children, took payment for her charity by stealing two of the children's shirts and a loaf of bread from the household. She also managed to extort money, and wreck the livelihood of a neighbouring poor family whose only living was gained from a horse and cart. When the head of the household passed away, Mary persuaded his widow, left with four children, that the eldest son, aged fifteen, was set on selling what little property his father had left, with the intent of absconding with the proceeds. Mary advised that to avoid this, the widow should sell the horse and cart and what little furniture she had, and leave Leeds with the cash. The widow, who was in fact stepmother to the fatherless children, followed Mary's instruction to the letter – and presumably paid a commensurate sum for it – and disappeared, leaving the children to go into the workhouse. Not to diminish their stepmother's part, Mary must have been fully aware of the fate that would befall those four children as a consequence of her actions.

While all the town's Charity Children in receipt of poor relief were taken into the workhouse, it was cold comfort for the young inmates; life in the workhouse was hard, especially for children. The first Leeds parish workhouse had opened in 1638 at the north-east corner of the junction of Lady Lane and Vicar Lane. Here, as in other workhouses, generations grew up in the shadow of an institution intended to be a form of social welfare for those with nothing. In practice, it was seen as a dark and terrible fate and a system which eroded all human dignity. The poor called the workhouses 'Bastilles' after the appalling prison in Paris destroyed during the Revolution of 1789. There was an enormous social stigma attached to ending up in the workhouse – a very public humiliation that everyone would have been aware of. Thousands of people lived in constant dread that some accident or illness would overtake them, leading to destitution and to that place where husbands were separated from their wives, and mothers from their children. Within these institutions, paupers were given profitless, pointless tasks such as breaking granite with a mallet or grinding animal bones by hand, while women scrubbed the floors, or sewed sails. Rules had to be obeyed to the letter on pain of harsh punishment, which included flogging and solitary confinement, and complaints about living conditions also invited punishment, as did lack of deference to the master. Dormitories regularly held up to seventy people, with beds of narrow bags of straw laid side by side and levels of cleanliness were low. It was noted in 1797 that the bedclothes in the Lady Lane Workhouse were 'scoured' once a year. Heating was minimal, even in the depths of winter, and paupers' heads were often shaved to protect against lice. Meals, such as they were, were often eaten in silence. While the able-bodied faced the daily grind of menial labour, for the elderly, the prospect of dying in a workhouse held out the grim possibility of a pauper's funeral in an unmarked grave or even worse, being despatched for anatomical dissection. Nobody went into the workhouse willingly.

While Mary was clearly responsible for some truly diabolical exploitation, she was still capable of incorporating petty thefts and frauds into her day, which ran to securing a free dinner. Finding herself one morning in The Shambles (the district of butchers shops which ran along Briggate from what would now be the junction with King Edward Street up to the entrance the County Arcade) on overhearing a man from Meadow Lane buying a leg of mutton with the instruction that it be delivered to his home, Mary decided she would intercept the purchase en route. She knew the direction the butcher's boy would have to take and, stationing herself on the Leeds Bridge, on seeing the boy approach with the parcelled up meat in his arms, she proceeded to scold him for taking too long a time about his errand and, manhandling the purchase from him, she said she would take it home to her master's kitchen herself, and gave the lad a thump on the back for good measure.

Needless to say, when the time came for the real cook in the Meadow Lane kitchen to prepare dinner, she was left wondering what had become of the delivery of meat. The butcher who had sold the mutton, after being berated by a decidedly less than satisfied customer, said that his delivery boy had been sent with it an hour since, but that the mutton had been taken off him by a woman purporting to be the customer's cook. The gentleman remembered having seen such a woman hanging around the shop earlier. The Batemans weren't destined to dine on stolen mutton that evening – the gentleman had recognised Mary and knew where she lived, and on being greeted by the cooking smells in the Bateman's kitchen, Mary was forced to make good on the cost of the stolen meat. Though she was spared the necessity of concocting a lie as to why her husband would find no supper on the table when he came home that evening, in hindsight she was fortunate that the wronged party had taken no legal action. Her later victims were less fortunate; Mary was free to carry on her life of crime.

Chapter 5

A Long Distance Dupe

Mary continued to read fortunes, mainly for young serving girls, many of whom she terrified into parting with what little savings they had. She also continued to employ the insights of the fictitious Miss Blythe, whose direction and advice she passed on to her dupes, wringing even more pennies from them. While the psychic industry remains a woefully unregulated one, then, as now, vulnerable people formed a credulous prey, believing claims of foretellings and clinging to predictions of a better future, presented under the guise of one who claims to have their best interests at heart. Though many do experience a beneficial measure of comfort and solace from psychic readings, tarot cards, astrological and clairvoyant predictions, even spiritual lifestyle gurus, there are those desperate for guidance and reassurance who can be held in the tightest grip of psychic addiction, cravenly acting on less than benign life-changing 'advice', usually centring on some cash transaction, and even more so in Mary's day.

The Scientific Revolution of the seventeenth century, centring on Isaac Newton in England, ought to have swept away the superstition of earlier centuries, but it hadn't. Few of the working class who were Mary's clients had anything resembling an enlightened education and to them, the mood swings of the economy and the ever-climbing natural death rate, were just as bewildering and terrifying as it had been to their ancestors.

Often employing the ruse of removing 'evil wishes', whether placed by a specific antagonist or by forces unseen, Mary's fraudulent and profitable exploitations now wholly centred on the instructions of Miss Blythe, who in spite of having 'no existence but in the artful mind and lying mouth of Mrs Bateman', nevertheless recommended a specific range of lucrative 'charms' that the desperately trusting fell for time and time again.

With regard to her own ministrations and those carried out on behalf of Miss Blythe, Mary could tentatively be placed into the category of folk healer, in England also known as 'cunning folk'. Their spells and charms as part of their profession stemmed from the Medieval period or earlier and carried through to the early twentieth century. Like Mary they were regarded as witches. While large numbers of ordinary people used the services of these white witches in lieu of expensive – and equally unreliable – doctors, it was all too easy for white witchcraft to slip to grey and then to black, the evil arts associated with Satan. There had been widespread persecution of them across Europe from the fifteenth to the eighteenth centuries, although the hysteria of Loudun in 1632 and Salem sixty years later, rarely showed itself in Britain. Most people, even magistrates, could tell a beneficent 'cunning woman' from a black witch and in any case, witchcraft in England was regarded as a felony, punished in extreme cases by hanging. It was not seen as devil-worship for which, in Europe and Scotland, the penalty was the stake.

Typically, the benefits that cunning folk offered their local community were facilitated by what they claimed to be their own magical powers, and operating in a competitive market where reputations and first impressions were very important. Perhaps Mary's ruse of the alter ego of Miss Blythe in some measure protected her against any potential backlash should her clientele prove dissatisfied, as her services were apparently directed by the instruction of another, professed to be highly skilled in such matters. White witches used spells and charms in order to combat malevolent witchcraft, to locate criminals, missing persons or stolen property, to tell fortunes, to heal, to seek out hidden treasure and to influence matters of the heart. In one example, a cunning man from Newcastle, Peter Banks, was charged in 1673–74 for offering to draw up a magical contract which promised to secure a presumably errant husband's fidelity for the term of one year. Cunning folk were often widely consulted with regard to health problems too, where both humans and their livestock were concerned. In the context of Mary's work as an abortionist, two hundred years earlier, those who practiced the 'dark arts' ran a serious risk. According to the sixteenth century *Examen of Witches*:

> 'Those midwives and wise women who are witches are in the habit of offering to Satan the little children which they deliver, and then of killing them … They do even worse; for they kill them while they are yet in their mothers' wombs. This practice is common to all witches.'

There may have been an element of power-seeking in Mary's control of her gullible clients, but her main motive was clearly greed. She used her literacy to write spells, usually symbols, grimoires or biblical quotations, giving the client hard 'proof' that the remedies were real. They all came, of course, at a cost, payable either to Mary herself or to be passed on to the mysterious, all-knowing Miss Blythe.

These particular charms, consisting of varying sums of money, supplied of course by the client, were sewn into small bags, and, once secreted as directed were not to be opened for a specific length of time, lest the magic be rendered ineffective. Invariably, when the bags were opened, they were found to contain worthless items equal to the weight of coin supposedly contained. By the time these discoveries were made, Mary was long on her way. One unfortunate client of Mary's, selected from the ranks of Leeds' youthful girls in domestic service, was persuaded that an 'evil wish' had been placed on her by an old beggar woman to whom she'd refused to give alms. After the initial provision of a pocket handkerchief for Miss Blythe, she then gave up five guineas to be sewn into five bags as an effective charm, along with handing over clothing to a corresponding value. Of course, Mary gave assurances that the money and clothing would be restored to her upon the cessation of the curse, but a few days before the appointed date when the bags were to have been opened, an anonymous gift of a fruit pie was received by this young woman, allegedly an offering from her sweetheart. While in appearance the pie appeared 'very nice', on sampling a slice with a fellow servant, the taste was found to be 'hot and offensive' and, her suspicions aroused, the girl took the pie straight to Mary for inspection. At that point, the girl still regarded her as a wise-woman and a trusted confidante.

Mary maintained that she knew nothing of such things, but that if she wrote to Miss Blythe she would be able to help. And so it proved. She told Mary that it was indeed fortunate that the pie had not been eaten as it was 'full of poison'. But then, Mary already knew that! Having failed to eliminate the gullible girl, when the appointed time came and the magic bags were finally opened it was discovered that the guineas had mysteriously changed to coppers and the clothing to rags. Needless to say, her dupe never saw Mary again.

Conveniently, Miss Blythe lived in Scarborough, a far enough distance from Leeds for Mary to maintain the pretence of her existence. It was also necessary for her to communicate by letter, giving Mary the opportunity of forging Miss Blythe's supposed replies and charging her clients for the postage into the bargain. One such correspondence entered into with Miss Blythe concerned the predicament of a widowed washerwoman called Judith Cryer.

In April 1807, Mrs Cryer had come to Mary in some distress concerning the behaviour of her eleven-year-old grandson. Mary had been recommended to Mrs Cryer by a Winifred Bond, who later testified at Mary's trial that she had been employed by Mary to run various errands for her, delivering letters and presumably acting as a recommending agent for Mary's services. It would later become apparent at Mary's trial that Winifred Bond was unable to read, a convenient deficiency from Mary's point of view, yet Winifred still had a tongue in her head, and this was presumably why Mary had later coerced this potential witness into leaving Leeds. She obligingly relocated to the outskirts of Keighley as she was afraid of the supernatural powers she supposed Mary to possess.

Thus began a masterly play on Judith Cryer's fears for her grandson's wayward inclinations, especially when the response received from Miss Blythe included a drawing of a gallows and hangman's noose, reinforcing the prediction that the grandson would be hanged before he reached the age of fourteen – unless, of course, Mrs Cryer stumped up four guineas in payment to Miss Blythe to avert the catastrophe. In view of Mrs Cryer's situation, Mary's exploitation of her was as shameless as any other she had undertaken. The occupation of washerwoman was largely the province of older women, often widows, trying to support themselves and their children. For those who could afford it washing was habitually 'sent out', especially in view of the time consuming and backbreaking aspects of laundry work before the advent of piped and heated water and domestic appliances; paying someone else to do the laundry was a top priority of many households when circumstances permitted. Though washing entailed a great deal of lifting and carrying, as well as the extraordinarily heavy job of wringing out sodden linen, in common with any other manual labour that was the province of the lower-classes, the wages were meagre. Somehow Mrs Cryer managed to scrape together what must have been an astronomical sum for a woman of her means, and at length an instruction arrived from Miss Blythe that three of the guineas were to be stitched into a leather bag – presumably the balance was pocketed by Mary as Miss Blythe's fee – and the bag then sewn into Mrs Cryer's bed, where it was to remain untouched until her grandson had attained the age of fourteen. Before the three-year interim was up however, Mary's later arrest and exposure caused Mrs Cryer to extract the bag from her bed, and on opening it found it to be empty. The three guineas of course had never been placed in the bag in the first place, and had long since been spent by Mary, who'd even had the audacity to make Mrs Cryer do her laundry free of charge for three months in order to defray the postal charges incurred in communing with Miss Blythe on her part!

While Mary was clearly consummate at the art of deception, she didn't always come out on top. A young man who had applied to her with the age old problem of having 'made a young woman a mother without making her a wife' was assured that a payment of 2 guineas would cover the cost of an effective charm that would remedy the situation. Perhaps if the expectant mother herself had applied to Mary the desired outcome would have been achieved, but the child duly arrived and the enraged father swore vengeance on Mary, forcing her to refund the monies he'd paid. But even here, Mary lied. Saying that she had no ready money in her possession, she claimed that she'd had the fortune to meet a mysterious 'man in black' on leaving her house one evening, and it was he who had given her the necessary coin to make good on her failed promise; a fortuitous and very usual occurrence on the streets of early nineteenth century Leeds!

Mary's extortions were not limited to exploiting the susceptible subjects identified by herself or those supplied by Winnifred Bond however, as she even extended her deceptions to her own family. One of Mary's brothers, having deserted from the Royal Navy, came with his wife to Leeds to lodge with the Batemans for a while to escape detection. If convicted, he would have faced the death penalty. The Navy was notorious for its harsh discipline; since a good many sailors in the seventeenth, eighteenth and early nineteenth centuries were pressed into service unwillingly, a firm hand was often needed to keep the crews in line. While flogging was frequently administered for lesser offences, deserters were hanged. After the destruction of the Franco-Spanish fleet at Trafalgar in 1805, the threat of invasion by France was seriously diminished. It could not be discounted entirely however, and the navy was still vital in maintaining trade, continuing its blockade of French ports and, after 1808, supplying Arthur Wellesley's army in Spain. Not a single sailor could be spared.

Mary must have found that the couple cramped her style somewhat, and conceived a plan to be rid of them both as well as turning a healthy profit from the exploitation of her house guests. Firstly, echoing her contrivance of John Bateman's unnecessary mercy dash to his healthy father's 'deathbed', Mary presented her sister-in-law with a forged letter from Newcastle stating that her own father's life was in the balance and that she should hurry to his side to receive his last blessing. Duped, as Bateman had been before her, Mary's sister-in-law got to Newcastle only to find her father in perfect health. The port on the Tyne was famous for its glass production at the time and its Literary and Philosophical Society was the envy of the north.

During his wife's absence, Mary put the time to good use, and began to work on her brother; she told him that not only had his wife been unfaithful to him but that she was busy running up extraordinary debts in his name. Furnishing him with the necessary ink and paper, Mary encouraged her brother to write to his wife telling her that the marriage was over and not to bother to return to Leeds. The lady was obviously made of sterner stuff as she did return, in spite of her husband's letter, and not only convinced him of the truth and of her constancy, but also of his sister's deceit, which became unquestionable when it was discovered that Mary had stolen all of their clothes from their travelling trunks and sold them for whatever money she could get. In the face of her brother's warranted indignation, Mary engineered the couple's hasty departure from Leeds by proceeding straight to the magistrate and informing on her brother as a deserter. Then she plumbed the depths even further when she wrote to her mother, telling her that her son had been apprehended as a deserter and that the sum of £10 was necessary to set him free. As any concerned mother would, Mrs Harker duly sent the money for her son's release. As well as informing on her brother and almost wrecking his marriage and causing untold distress and financial hardship to their mother, Mary had managed to turn a healthy profit from the whole sorry episode.

Mary also ran a long distance dupe on two serving girls whose move to Manchester she had engineered. Having been under Mary's influence for some time, along with several of their friends who had all been persuaded of her powers of foretelling in matters of the heart, one girl had even resorted to stealing various articles from her mother, including a large family Bible, to satisfy Mary's demands. However, when these extortions had reached such a point that Mary was concerned she might be discovered, she contrived to send both girls, at different times, to seek a position in service in Manchester. The Cottonopolis was growing at an alarming rate in these years, swallowing up the outlying villages which are now its suburbs. The first cotton mill had been opened there by Richard Arkwright in 1780 and the city's slums were home to thousands of cellar-dwelling Irish. Keeping up a correspondence with each of them, Mary managed a long distance extortion of clothing and belongings that meant the desperate girls were virtually naked. The likelihood of the pair accidentally meeting in the city with its 70,000 population seemed remote but

Mary had nevertheless included a codicil concerning the procurement of a suitable husband. Both were instructed that if they were to happen to meet one another in Manchester they must under no circumstances exchange a word, lest the charm put in place be broken. But one day, by chance, they did meet in the street, and in spite of Mary's threats regarding fraternisation, the pair broke down in tears and revealed identical tales of woe. Realising they had both been wholly taken in by Mary, they wrote to their friends back in Leeds, who in this instance got back the money and clothing that Mary had coerced from them, though needless to say the promised husbands never materialised.

In 1807, in view of the continuing exposures of Mary's increasing frauds, the Batemans were forced to move yet again, this time to Meadow Lane, south of the river Aire in a populous south-western suburb of Leeds called Holbeck. While there, another poisoning-related incident involving the family of a long unemployed cloth-dresser named Gosling was brought to the notice of the local surgeon, and while the circumstances and the motive for the attempted poisoning are not clear, in view of Mary's track record the finger of suspicion was afterwards firmly pointed in her direction.

Joseph Gosling and his wife and four children, who were living in dire straits, returned to their house one day to find a small cake on the kitchen table. The mother and children immediately tasted the surprising though welcome free gift of food, and though it had a 'very keen and pungent taste', nevertheless, they ate several mouthfuls and soon began to feel very ill. Thankfully the local surgeon, a Mr Atkinson, was summoned and by the timely administration of emetics saved the lives of the entire family. As for the fateful cake, on inspection it was found to contain a large quantity of arsenic. While the description of the taste of the cake, and the rapid subsequent ill effects on those who had eaten it were clear indicators of the presence of poison, Mr Atkinson may well have carried out some additional rudimentary toxicological tests – similar tests of a physical nature would later be presented as evidence at Mary Bateman's trial.

Chemistry had spectacularly come to the aid of forensic science in 1752 when the first of such tests had secured a conviction in a case of poisoning by arsenic. In that year, Mary Blandy, acting on the instructions of her lover, fed her father arsenic trioxide. The powder Mary stirred into her father's tea and gruel every day made him so ill that he would stay up all night with vomiting and stomach pains. After a few attempts she eventually killed him, but not before he realised his daughter's true intent. Her father's love was such that his main concern during his final days was not that he would die but that Mary should not hang for his murder. The poison she had used was a white powder, and it was a Dr Addington who identified it. Having treated Francis Blandy, Addington suspected arsenic was the substance that had poisoned him and conducted a series of physical tests to prove his point. When he put a sample of the powder Mary had given her father into cold water, for instance, part of it remained on the water's surface, but most of it stayed on the bottom undissolved – the same results apparent when a known sample of arsenic was similarly tested. Additionally, when Addington tossed the powder onto a red-hot piece of iron, it did not burn, but sublimated (that is transformed directly from a solid to the gaseous state), rising up in garlic-smelling white clouds just as arsenic did. Addington argued at Mary Blandy's trial that these results proved the powder employed was, in fact, arsenic, and the forensic evidence he provided helped to convince the jury that Mary had poisoned her father. While of course the results of Addington's early forensic tests were not definitive and would be regarded as rudimentary by today's standards, and neither were they specific to arsenic alone, the jury nevertheless agreed with Addington's findings, and this was the first time any court had accepted toxicological evidence in an arsenic-poisoning case. Sentenced to death for her father's murder she was hanged on 6 April 1752 in the castle yard at Oxford, seemingly more concerned with preserving her modesty than with her imminent death. Mary's last request was that, for the sake of decency, she should not be hoisted too high, concerned that the young men in the crowd would look up her skirts. As for the fate of the lady's coercive lover, he escaped before he could stand trial, but died later that year.

In the case of the Gosling family, if Mary Bateman was indeed responsible, while her motives were unclear, it is testament to her tarnished character that the blame was laid squarely with her.

It comes as no surprise that by the following year, in 1808, the Batemans had again moved and were now living in Camp Field off Water Lane, an area of high density housing close to the flax mill of Marshall & Benyon, the same mill which had suffered the serious fire back in 1796 and so mercenarily exploited by Mary in her 'charitable' endeavours. Here ninety-two pairs of back-to-back houses occupied a field called Bar Croft, measuring 75 yards by 125 yards. Amongst the many occupying this slum, Mary found a new and impressionable neighbour to exploit in the wife of James Snowden. Whether Mrs Snowden already believed in prophecy or the notion was implanted by Mary's powerful suggestion, her fears centring on a presentiment of the drowning of one of her children were certainly exacerbated by Mary to increase her gains. Whatever the origins of Mrs Snowden's premonition, Mary assured her that Miss Blythe would be able to help. Miss Blythe, who had now apparently moved to Thirsk, still far enough away to preserve the pretence of her reality, wrote advising that in order to save the child from a watery grave, Mr Snowden's silver pocket watch must be sewn, by Mary, into the Snowden's bed, in addition to the sum of twelve guineas stitched into the mattress. The Snowdens could of course later extricate the watch and the money, but only once the charm had worked.

In view of the monies already laid out, Mary obviously saw an opportunity for further exploitation, and increased Mrs Snowden's fears by telling her that Miss Blythe had also warned that unless the family moved to Bowling, a village on the outskirts of Bradford then opening up to the iron trade, then the Snowdens' daughter would end up a prostitute working the streets of Leeds. While the bed containing the preventive monetary charms and silver pocket watch could be taken with them, Mary persuaded husband and wife that it would be expedient to leave a considerable amount of their property in their Leeds house, and leave the key with the Batemans.

Later, now relocated in Bradford, the Snowdens expressed a wish to tear open the bed and retrieve the watch and money. The request of course posed a decided problem for Mary. She wrote back advising that, in line with Miss Blythe's instructions, enough time had not yet elapsed, and in the face of her imminent exposure, Mary also told the Snowdens that before the guineas and watch were removed, the entire family would need to take a special 'dose' in order to render the magic of the concealed charms powerful enough to prevent their son from drowning and their daughter's descent into the life of a streetwalker. That Mary had in mind the poisoning of the Snowdens in order to prevent the discovery of her fraud is obvious; it would also have cleared the way for her to grab all the possessions still remaining in the Snowden's vacant Leeds home to which she still held the key. The allotted time for the administration of the dose, divined by Miss Blythe, was set for the end of October 1808. Presumably, this would have taken the form of a powder, which Mary assured was currently being prepared by Miss Blythe, that would have been sent to the Snowdens along with specific instructions as to how it should be administered. The plan of course was that effectively, the Snowdens would be responsible for poisoning themselves. However, the threat to the family was averted at the eleventh hour by the exposure of Mary's part in the poisoning of another held under Miss Blythe's influence and the timely publicity surrounding her arrest for her part in the death of Rebecca Perigo, brought about by Mary in the May of the previous year. This was the crime for which she would be tried, convicted and hanged.

Chapter 6

'My dear Friend...'

On the evening of the 22 October 1808, Mr Snowden had the good fortune to call into a public house in Bradford and overhear a discussion about an article in the *Leeds Mercury* newspaper. Under the heading 'Witchcraft, Murder and Credulity' the report said:

> 'A plot, accompanied by most unprecedented instances of credulity that ever engaged public attention, was on Monday developed before the Magistrates, at the Rotation-office in Leeds.'

Detailing the arrest the previous day of Mary Bateman, apprehended by the Chief Constable of Leeds on a charge of fraud, the article elaborated on the details of her exploitation of a married couple named Perigo, who lived at Bramley, an already industrialised area on the outskirts of Leeds. It rang loud alarm bells with Snowden, who hurried home to tell his wife. As the article alluded to the similar recommendations of a 'Miss Blythe', namely the stitching of money into the Perigos' bed, the Snowdens promptly tore open their own bedding only to find that the twelve guineas and the silver pocket watch which had purportedly been stitched in by Mary Bateman had incredibly changed into pieces of coal. On this discovery, Snowden hurried back to Leeds to find that their house, left in Mary's care, had been stripped bare. It took no great powers of deduction to identify the culprit. Getting a search warrant to enter the Batemans' premises, some of the Snowdens' missing effects and household belongings were found to have been removed to the Batemans' home, the other of the Snowdens' missing items presumably already disposed of by direct sale or pledged at the pawnbrokers.

Mary's luck had finally run out. Her arrest had been brought about by a complaint lodged by William Perigo, a cloth merchant who, before her death, had lived with his wife Rebecca in Bramley, approximately four miles north-west of Leeds city centre. A childless, middle aged couple, the Perigos were comfortably off, though William had become increasingly concerned about Rebecca's chest palpitations, described as 'flacking' or 'fluttering in the breast' which occurred whenever she lay down. As well as this physical ailment, she was also having psychological problems, claiming to be haunted by a black dog and other spirits. Though the particular manifestation of a black dog may seem peculiar, the phenomenon is in fact an age old superstition; feared as portents of death, tales of spectral hounds are legion throughout the British Isles, and known by different names in different parts of the country. In Norfolk they are Shucks, Gallytorts in Suffolk, the Trash marauds in Lancashire and Padfoots are seen in Staffordshire, but in Yorkshire they were, and still are, known as 'Barghests'.

Though a cure was sought through conventional medicine, Rebecca was told by her physician, a Dr Curzley who was clearly as superstitious as his patient, that she was under some sort of spell, and that he could do nothing to help her. At Whitsun 1806, which that year fell on 25 May, Rebecca Perigo's niece, Sarah Stead, who lived in Leeds, came to visit her aunt and uncle in Bramley. Rebecca complained to her niece of the 'fluttering in her side' which she supposed was the result of an 'evil wish' which had been laid upon her. Rebecca was just about to celebrate her forty-sixth birthday, on 29 May and, as William Perigo affirmed at Mary Bateman's trial, in twenty years of marriage his wife had always enjoyed a very good state of health and 'was never confined a week to her bed on account of illness since they were married'. It would seem likely that Rebecca was suffering heart palpitations, in all probability brought on by the anxiety and stress caused by the unseen curse to which she attributed the ailment to in the first place. It was a vicious circle of fear.

In the light of her aunt's discomforts, Sarah innocently suggested the services of Mary Bateman, whose reputation she knew, and who she thought might be able to rid Rebecca of the troubling spirits that were possessing her, and presumably remedy her physical ailments at the same time. Sarah actually called on Mary then still living at the aptly-named Black Dog Yard the same day after her visit to Bramley, and recounted how she'd found her aunt 'very low and poorly' and that while William had already enlisted the services of a country doctor, he had been told that his wife was suffering as a consequence of the evil wish cast upon her. Mary must have been laughing all the way to the bank at the prospect presented by Rebecca Perigo's ill health. She confidently claimed to have cured many others who'd suffered similar chest pains to those afflicting Rebecca, and she assured Sarah Stead that she knew of a lady who could cure her aunt, although she didn't mention the name of Miss Blythe at this juncture, and assured the Perigos' niece that she would write the necessary letter and have an answer within a fortnight. However, she would require a flannel petticoat, or any other under-garment worn next to her aunt's skin, to send on to her confidant in order to assist with the removal of the spell. From this article of clothing, Miss Blythe would be able to 'collect a knowledge of her disorder.'

After some weeks' delay – perhaps the Perigos were deliberating over the use of Mary's services, or perhaps Rebecca's health had temporarily improved – a meeting was arranged between William Perigo and Mary toward the end of July, outside the Black Dog pub. A flannel petticoat of Mrs Perigo's was duly handed over, to be sent to Miss Blythe in

Scarborough by that night's post and, this being a Saturday, William should call back on the Tuesday or Wednesday following for Miss Blythe's reply and instructions. We can assume that Mary added a new flannel petticoat to her wardrobe at this point.

When William returned to Black Dog Yard the following week, Mary showed him the forged reply from Miss Blythe, directing that Mary should go to the Perigos' house in Bramley, and employing the tried and tested ploy, stitch into their bed four guinea notes enclosed in bags; Miss Blythe had enclosed the notes with her letter. One should go into each corner of the Perigos' bed, where they must be left untouched for a period of eighteen months in order to lift the curse afflicting Rebecca. To defray Miss Blythe's cash outlay, William was to give Mary four guinea notes of his own in exchange, to be sent back to Miss Blythe accordingly, with the further instruction that Miss Blythe would only continue with the undertaking on the faithful promise that Mrs Perigo would not discuss the on-going situation with anyone else, lest the charm be broken.

Obviously at this point Mary was not certain of the worth of her victims, and how much money she could get from them, so she engineered a ruse to be left alone in their house so that she could assess their living standards and make a mental inventory of their belongings. Having arranged with William that she would come to the family home on 4 August to carry out Miss Blythe's instructions, it was agreed that his wife would meet Mary on the Kirkstall Bridge, a little over a mile from the Perigos' home in Bramley. However, when Rebecca turned up at the appointed time and place Mary was nowhere to be seen, and for good reason; she had already made her way over to Bramley and upon Mary's unaccompanied arrival at the Perigos' door, a surprised and concerned William set off out to look for his wife. As Mary had planned, she was conveniently left alone in the house for a considerable time.

When the Perigos finally returned together, presumably Mary concocted some plausible nonsense for having missed Rebecca on the Kirkstall Bridge and she got down to the business of sleight of hand. Producing the four guinea notes sent by Miss Blythe, she had William Perigo examine them before they were switched and stitched into four silk bags, Mary having substituted ordinary pieces of paper for the guinea notes that Miss Blythe had supplied. These were pocketed along with the four guinea notes that Perigo had given her in exchange for Miss Blythe's supposed outlay. As Mary had the Perigos themselves open their mattress, and place each of the silk bags with their worthless contents into the respective corners of the bed, they had no reason to believe they were being defrauded. The first deceit accomplished, a grateful William accompanied Mary on part of her way home, she leaving him with the instruction that he should call on her occasionally at Black Dog Yard whenever he was in Leeds to see if any further instructions had been received from Miss Blythe.

Within a fortnight, another letter was indeed 'received' from Miss Blythe, and delivered to the Perigos by one of the Bateman sons. It was unsealed, and stated that within a few days, Mary was to visit the Perigos to undertake some more 'protective' measures, namely to hammer over their threshold two pieces of iron shaped as horse shoes. It was however essential that William buy the necessary iron, but under no circumstances should the metal be sourced from Bramley. In addition, they were to be nailed into place not with a hammer, but with the back part of a pair of pincers. The self-same pincers were then to be posted by Mary directly to Miss Blythe in Scarborough. Whether this performance was merely designed to keep up the impetus of Miss Blythe's own special brand of magic, or whether Mary was simply in need of a new pair of pincers we cannot know!

When Mary arrived in Bramley a few days later, William had failed to obtain the necessary shaped iron, and had to go to Stanningley, a neighbouring village, to fetch it. On his return the 'shoes' were nailed into place according to instruction, Mary taking with her the pincers for supposed despatch to Scarborough where they were to remain in Miss Blythe's possession for a stipulated period of eighteen months, the same time-frame allotted for the removal of the 'guinea notes' stitched into the Perigos' bed.

A few weeks after the threshold charms had been put up, about the middle of October, William Perigo received another letter from Miss Blythe, delivered by the post boy from Leeds. It read:

> 'My dear Friend --- You must go down to Mary Bateman's at Leeds, on Tuesday next, and carry two guinea notes with you and give her them, and she will give you other two that I have sent to her from Scarborough, and you must buy me a small cheese about six or eight pound weight, and it must be of your buying, for it is for a particular use, and it is to be carried down to Mary Bateman's, and she will send it to me by the coach -- This letter is to be burned when you have done reading it.'

The last instruction with regard to burning the letter was one consistently repeated in all future correspondences received from Miss Blythe. Though sometimes the manner in which the letter was to be burned varied - 'with a candle', 'in straw on the hearth of your wife' even 'at some public house in Leeds' where William was to buy a pint of beer first, the end result was the same, Mary achieving the destruction of incriminating evidence by the very hands of those she was swindling.

At the beginning of December 1806, another letter was received, with a request for more money:

> 'My dear Friend --- You must go down to Mary Bateman's on Tuesday next, and take four guineas notes with you and she will give you other four in exchange for them, which I have sent, and when you read this letter it must be burned.'

From the time this letter was received through to March 1807, many further correspondences were sent, supposedly from Miss Blythe, roughly every fortnight, either carried by Mary Bateman's son or arriving in the post. The letters demanded the surrender of various articles of furniture, clothing and other property, and of course money, all through the agency of Mary Bateman, and all to be sent on to Scarborough during the eighteen-month period stipulated by Miss Blythe. During this period, the Perigos handed over in the region of £70 in hard cash, and on each payment, William received silk bags into which he believed Mary had stitched what purported to be the coins and notes he had made over, and these were duly sewn into the Perigos' bed as before. With regard to the household items extorted from the Perigos during this period, at Mary's trial these were listed as amounting to the following:

One Goose
Two Pairs of Men's Shoes
A Goose Pye (pie)
A Tea Caddy
Several Shirts
A Counterpane (bed covering)
A Piece of Woollen Cloth
A Silk Shawl
A Light Coloured Gown Skirt
A Light Coloured Cotton Gown
Two Pillow Slips
Six Strokes* of Malt
A Quantity of Tea and Sugar
Two or Three Hundred Eggs
A Pair of Worsted Stockings
A Pair of new Shoes
A Pair of Black Silk Stockings
Three Yards of Knaresbro' Linen Cloth
Ten Stones of Malt (63.5kg)
A Piece of Beef
Three Bottles of Spirits

A New Waistcoat	Two Table Cloths
Sixty Pounds of Butter (a little over 27kg)	Two Barrels (327 litres)
Seven Strokes* of Meal	Two Napkins

*A 'stroke' or 'strike' was a unit of volume used for dry measure and equivalent to 2 bushels, that is 16 imperial gallons - a little under 73 litres.

Miss Blythe's demands continued however. In March 1807 she wrote:

> 'My dear Friends. – I will be obliged to you if you will let me have half-a-dozen of your china, three silver spoons, half-a-pound of tea, two pounds of loaf sugar, and a tea canister to put the tea in, or else it will not do -- I durst not drink out of my own china. You must burn this with a candle.'

Whether the Perigos' resources were exhausted, or they had begun to doubt the powers of the heavily exacting Miss Blythe, when the china, silverware and other items failed to arrive by April, Miss Blythe put pen to paper again, pressing the requests made in the March letter which had not been forthcoming, along with a demand for a new bed and bedding as she was unable to sleep in her own bed due to the battle she was having with the spirits that had taken over Rebecca Perigo. Presumably, these same spirits had previously had some detrimental effect on Miss Blythe's china and spoons too, as her March letter mentioned. Upping her demands, Miss Blythe wrote again to her 'dear Friends' that she would:

> '...be obliged to you if you will buy me a camp bedstead, bed and bedding, a blanket, a pair of sheets, and a long bolster must come

> from your house. You need not buy the best feathers, common ones will do. I have laid on the floor for three nights, and I cannot lay on my own bed owing to the planets being so bad concerning your wife, and I must have one of your buying or it will not do. You must bring down the china, the sugar, the caddy, the three silver spoons, and the tea at the same time when you buy the bed, and pack them up altogether. My brother's boat will be up in a day or two, and I will order my brother's boatman to call for them all at Mary Bateman's, and you must give Mary Bateman one shilling for the boatman, and I will place it to your account. Your wife must burn this as soon as it is read or it will not do.'

At this point the Perigos' faith must have revived, along with their flagging finances as, accompanied by Mary, William dutifully purchased a bed and bedstead from the shop of a Mr Dobbin and the other items from a Mr Musgrave, both in Kirkgate in Leeds, at a total cost of £16 including the required set of china and various other items. All of the purchases were then delivered to Mr Sutton's, at the Lion & Lamb Inn on Kirkgate, there to await collection by the boatman of Miss Blythe's brother. At least one person's suspicions were however aroused at this time, as Mr Dobbin, from whom the bed and bedstead had been purchased, commented that 'it was a strange thing to send a bed so far' and at this point we should perhaps examine the susceptibility of the Perigos, as their submission to Miss Blythe's demands seemed gullible in the extreme. Indeed, the judge presiding over Mary's trial put forward that 'it is impossible not to be struck with wonder at the extraordinary credulity of Wm. Perigo, which neither the loss of his property, the death of his wife, and his own severe sufferings could dispel.' Yet, in spite of William's 'uncommon want of judgement' it must be borne in mind that Mary's adeptness in identifying the psychological weaknesses of those ripe for exploitation, and her powers of persuasion were such that the Perigos were merely the latest in a long line of others who had fallen victim to her machinations. Clearly, Mary was a supreme exponent of the art of capitalising on the superstitious beliefs that people still firmly held in the early nineteenth century and used this to rob the unwary of all their worldly possessions. As the Perigo affair was to prove, Mary was certainly adept at playing the 'long game'.

As the deception wore on, Mary must have been astute enough to realise that either the couple were out of cash, or harbouring a growing suspicion, as she now brought into play the stratagem that was her hallmark. When the cover for her frauds looked to be wearing thin, to avoid discovery and exposure, Mary's victims had to be eliminated. To this end, Miss Blythe wrote another letter paving the way for Mary to start poisoning William and Rebecca Perigo, and to give the lie some additional bite, and exacerbate those fears of the Perigos which had seen them fall into Mary's clutches in the first place, Miss Blythe warned that death was imminent, should her instructions not be fully complied with. At the end of April 1807, the following letter arrived:

> 'My dear Friends --- I am sorry to tell you you will take an illness in the month of May next, either t'one or both of you, but I think both, but the works of God must have its course. You will escape the chambers of the grave; though you seem to be dead, yet you will live. Your wife must take half-a-pound of honey down from Bramley to Mary Bateman's at Leeds, and it must remain there till you go down yourself, and she will put in such like stuff as I have sent from Scarbro' to her, and she will put it in when you come down, and see her yourself, or it will not do. You must eat pudding for six days, and you must put in such like stuff as I have sent to Mary Bateman from Scarbro', and she will give your wife it, but you must not begin to eat of this pudding while I let

> you know. If ever you find yourself sickly at any time, you must take each of you a teaspoonful of this honey; I will remit twenty pounds to you on the 20th day of May, and it will pay a little of what you owe. You must bring this down to Mary Bateman's, and burn it at her house, when you come down next time.'

Obviously the last instruction to burn this particularly incriminating correspondence in Mary's presence was a very necessary precaution in view of the instructions contained in it and the plan of poisoning that Mary had initiated.

'The chambers of the grave' were indeed to prove prophetic words. A compliant Rebecca went to see Mary with half a pound of honey, and as the letter instructed, Mary mixed into it some of the special 'medicine' that Miss Blythe had prepared. Rebecca left with six packets of powder, marked for daily incorporation into the Perigos' puddings, Mary reminding her that they must be used in the precise manner directed, or they would *all* die, Mary and Miss Blythe included.

On 5 May, another letter arrived from Miss Blythe, instructing the Perigos to start eating the powder laced puddings on 11 May – but observing the culinary caveat that on each of the six days no more pudding than was sufficient for them both should be prepared, and that nobody else was allowed to eat any. If there were any leftovers these should be disposed of immediately. Miss Blythe was also clear that should either William or Rebecca become 'sickly', under no circumstances were they to call a doctor as he would not be able to help them. Finally, this letter, like all the others, was to be burned.

Not only had Mary Bateman succeeded in acquiring a great number of goods and a considerable amount of money from the Perigos, the couple were now about to conveniently poison themselves and destroy all the written incriminating evidence substantiating Mary's involvement into the bargain.

On 11 May, a Monday, William and Rebecca dutifully began the regimen of pudding eating. Initially they suffered no ill effects, however on the sixth day, the quantity of powder in the packet marked for use on Saturday being five to six times larger than the previous doses, Rebecca made a small cake along with their pudding, to use up all the powder. On tasting the cake, William commented to his wife that it 'tasted very keen' and that 'if the pudding tasted as bad he would not eat it'. True to his word, after one mouthful he found the pudding so nauseating that he could eat no more. Rebecca on the other hand, clearly keen to swallow what she thought would be the resolution to all her problems, managed three or four mouthfuls. Unable to eat any more, she went to take the unfinished pudding to the cellar; on her way however she was seized with the 'most violent vomitings'. Yet to Rebecca, this sudden downturn in her state of health was indicative of the illness predicted in Miss Blythe's letter, and accordingly she broke out the special honey, a teaspoon of which was to be taken by them both in the event of sickness. William ate two spoonfuls, while Rebecca took six or seven. Predictably they both rapidly took a turn for the worse. William described a 'violent heat' coming out of his mouth which was very sore and that his lips turned black, accompanied by a violent headache 'twenty times worse than a common head-ache' and his vision disturbed so that 'everything appeared green to him'. Rebecca, who of course had eaten far more of the poison than her husband, vomited incessantly for twenty-four hours, but would not hear of a doctor being called as this would be going against Miss Blythe's express instructions, and the charm would be broken. Instead, she ate even more of the honey. While Rebecca's symptoms initially mirrored William's, they quickly became more extreme; her tongue swelled so that she was unable to close her mouth and she complained of a constant thirst. As the poison progressed through her system and the symptoms worsened, her strength failing over a week of agonising torment and suffering, on Sunday 24 May, Rebecca Perigo died. Yet even on her deathbed, she was still under Miss Blythe's influence, her last words to her husband being that he not be 'rash' with Mary Bateman, and that he himself should keep the appointment with Miss Blythe, whom Rebecca was supposed to have met at Mary Bateman's house the following day.

While the self-administration of the poison Mary had supplied was carefully timed so that the meeting with the mythical Miss Blythe would never take place, and indeed the entire fraud perpetrated against the Perigos would never come to light, the fact that William Perigo had survived the attempt on his life now posed a serious dilemma for Mary; but not one that her resourcefulness, or so she thought, could fail to resolve.

Chapter 7

The End of a Crooked Road

Despite his wife's entreaties, shortly before she died, William Perigo took it upon himself to send for a surgeon from Leeds, a Mr Chorley, but as word of Mrs Perigo's death reached him before he actually arrived in Bramley, it wasn't until the day after his wife's death that Perigo paid a visit to the surgeon himself. On examining his patient, and taking into account the symptoms described, Mr Chorley drew the conclusion that poison had been ingested. As a means of proof, Mr Chorley suggested that some of the flour used in the last fateful pudding be made up into a paste and fed to a chicken to see what harm befell it. Whether or not the flour used was untainted, or the test subject had a lucky escape, the chicken suffered no ill effects from the experiment. However, a cat which had been experimentally fed some of the cooked pudding (by the Perigos' neighbours) did die immediately, and though Mr Chorley's suspicions were clearly aroused, no further steps were taken to ascertain the real cause of Rebecca's death at that time, and no autopsy was performed on her body. Chorley did later perform an autopsy on the body of a dog which had died as a result of being fed pills and a solution made from honey that the couple were directed to take. There was poison in the animal's stomach.

After his wife's death, William went into Leeds to tell Mary that Rebecca had died. Mary's surprising and admonishing reaction was that Rebecca's life would have been preserved had she 'licked up' all of the special honey as directed in Miss Blythe's letter. When William inferred that it was in fact the honey that had caused his wife's death, an angry Mary remonstrated that if he would bring her what was left of the jar of honey she would 'lick it up before his eyes and satisfy him'. What she would have done had William called her bluff we can only guess at, though she would have thought of something! Incredibly, even after his wife's death, William Perigo seemed willing to continue his subjugation to Miss Blythe and not long after this confrontation, he received another letter from the lady, commiserating on Rebecca's death but nonetheless blaming her demise, and the threat to her own and Mary Bateman's lives, on Rebecca having 'touched of those things which I ordered her not to', presumably the 'money' stitched into the Perigo's bed. Miss Blythe also said that Rebecca would rise from the grave to stroke her husband's face with her right hand, and that William would 'lose the use of one side', but that Miss Blythe would pray for him. Of course, he should also burn the letter immediately after having read it. Was Mary paving the way for another murder attempt attributable to a stroke perhaps? She certainly had a problem on her hands with William having survived her previous attempt, and he had unwittingly thwarted another bid in not telling Mary he was taking a curative trip to the spa of Buxton on the instruction of his surgeon, Mr Chorley. It may be asked however as to why William chose not to avail himself of one of the more northerly spas, resorts such as Harrogate, Ilkley and around Croft-on-Tees, or even those in Leeds itself like Quarry Hill. Perhaps he preferred to distance himself somewhat from the recent traumas culminating in the death of his wife.

On his return from taking the waters, Mary upbraided the widower for not telling her that he was going to Buxton, as, had she known he was to take a journey, she would have would have given him a bottle, the contents of which 'would have cured him on the road'. Assuredly the contents of that bottle would have done little to 'cure' William Perigo.

After returning to Bramley, he continued to receive letters from Miss Blythe, full of renewed demands. Her powers of perception were great indeed, as in looking at William's 'planet' she had seen his return from Buxton, and was sorry that if only he had stayed a few days longer, he would have had the opportunity of meeting Miss Blythe there herself.

All of Mary's nefarious deeds notwithstanding, she must be congratulated for the power of her imagination, as the incident she concocted to explain the necessity of Miss Blythe's fictional trip to Buxton was outlandish to say the least. Apparently Miss Blythe had been injured when she and her brother had been thrown from their open carriage when the horse drawing it took fright at the sight of a hot air balloon! Astutely covering all the possible loopholes in her story, Mary was even meticulous enough to make sure that the next letter received from Miss Blythe was headed and dated as being written from Buxton, the small matter of the absence of a Buxton postmark explained away by Miss Blythe having enclosed her letter with another bound for Bradford, the letter to William having been posted on from there.

In the Buxton letter, Miss Blythe directed William to take one of his wife's gowns to Mary Bateman in Leeds, from whence it would be delivered to her in Buxton, though clearly the dress he chose did not meet with Mary's approval, as in the next letter received in October, Miss Blythe berated William for sending her 'such a shabby gown', especially when she knew he had one better; apparently the 'planets' enabled Miss Blythe to assess the contents of a dead woman's wardrobe too. Requesting instead one of Mrs Perigo's best gowns, along with a petticoat and a skirt, Miss Blythe also required the Perigo family Bible be sent to her for her 'to sit upon in the coach' when she returned from Buxton; the reason for which remains a puzzle. We can assume that the family Bible extorted by Mary from the serving girl forced to steal from her mother, back in the days when she was casting fortunes while living in Marsh Lane, had long since been pawned.

Two further letters received by William in October contained various requests for 'a guinea and a half to buy a waggon load of coals' specifically to be purchased from a 'Mr Fenton's, near Leeds' in addition to 'one stone and a half of flour; four ounces of tea, a pound or two of sugar, and a quantity of eggs' - one of which was to be blown and a guinea note inserted into the empty shell 'for a particular use' – presumably lining Mary's pocket.

Miss Blythe's missives continued until September 1808, latterly defending Mary Bateman's good character and with hollow promises of the return of the monies laid out. Finally, William Perigo investigated the silken bags which had been stitched into his and Rebecca's bed – perhaps he was understandably short of money. On 19 October, he steeled himself and opened them all. He must have recalled all the occasions when he had received from Mary a silk bag into which he believed her to have stitched what purported to be the coins and notes he had made over on the instruction of Miss Blythe. One wonders whether, in his heart of hearts, he was entirely surprised to find that inside each bag, where he expected to find guinea notes he found only scrap paper, and halfpennies and farthings where he expected to find gold coins. Even worse, the four bags containing the guinea notes that were the first to have been stitched into the bed were missing entirely. Now the game was really up, and William Perigo went to Leeds to confront Mary Bateman.

Of course this wasn't the first time that Mary had been faced with an accusation of deception, and her predictable retort to William with regard to the now worthless contents of the silk bags was that 'you have opened them too soon', breaking the magic of the charm and causing the contents to be magically changed into valueless coppers and paper. William responded 'I think it is too late,' and said he would return the following morning in company with two or three men to settle the matter. Though alarmed, Mary must have thought that her powers of manipulation might yet still have some effect, and begged that a private meeting be arranged, on the bank of the Leeds and Liverpool canal on the following morning, where she assured William that 'she would satisfy him'.

Though poorer, William Perigo was nevertheless now wiser. He agreed to the meeting with Mary the following day, but had no intention of going alone. This was a prudent precaution because as the canal side meeting played out, it was clear that Mary had intended to eliminate William once and for all. One of the two men he had asked to accompany him was William Duffield, the Chief Constable of Leeds. Clearly, Perigo was by this time highly suspicious of the ever-growing demands of Miss Blythe and her ingénue go-between. As a man who had once been of some means, it was natural that he should inform the authorities; Mary had bitten off more than she could chew this time. Both men kept a discreet distance but when Mary discovered their presence she feigned an attack of vomiting and accused William Perigo of having given her a bottle of poisonous liquid, which she had in fact brought along herself. During her examination before the Leeds magistrate, Mary alleged that William had given her the bottle the night before her arrest, and while her husband 'did never take any of it' she did and 'was very ill after it'. On later analysis the bottle was found to contain a mixture of oatmeal and arsenic, and was presumably intended to silence William Perigo for good. Chief Constable Duffield was not impressed by Mary's charade however, and promptly took her into custody.

The mechanics of Mary's arrest and detention are far from clear. *The Extraordinary Life* skates over them, presumably because its readers would know how the system worked. The Borough Corporation Act and the later Constabulary Act meant that more modern police forces were set up, sweeping away the old. We know that the Chief Constable appointed in 1836 to head up the new force in Leeds already held a similar position but the size and exact nature of his old force is not specified. Mary would have been taken into custody by Constables of the Watch, 'Charlies' as they were known because the post had been set up in the reign of Charles II. These men were barely literate, some of them not physically up to the job of chasing criminals and they were under the control of Duffield, whose job was honorary and unpaid. There were no women in any police force as early as this, although for delicate jobs, such as searching Mary's person, a local civilian female was probably drafted in.

William then accompanied Duffield to Mary's house where a search revealed many of the items bought by the Perigos and supposedly sent on to Miss Blythe in Scarborough were in fact in Mary's possession, amongst them the bed, tea caddy and set of china purchased in the April of the previous year, along with various other items including articles of clothing, two or three hat boxes, some sacking in which malt had been delivered and a pair of pincers – presumably those used to hammer home the horseshoe shaped pieces of iron over Perigos' front door, one of the earliest charms recommended by Miss Blythe.

Clearly, there was no way that Mary could talk herself out of this damning predicament. She was brought before the Leeds magistrates the following day charged with fraud, and after undergoing several long examinations she 'in part confessed her delinquency, and admitted that there was no such person as Miss Blythe in existence, but that the whole was a mere phantom, conjured up to forward her vile purposes'. It was clear however that she was guilty of more than fraud, and Mary was held pending the investigation into the suspicious death of Rebecca Perigo. The magistrate, whose name is not given in *The Extraordinary Life*, was a local gentleman who worked, as did many law officers, in an unpaid capacity for the good of the community. Mary had no defence counsel, either at this arraignment or her later trial and there were no rules governing how evidence was obtained. She clearly underwent hours of questioning and only had her wits to keep her going.

Though Mary was arrested toward the end of October 1808, it was 6 January 1809 before the murder charges were formally laid, after which time she was committed to York Castle Gaol where she awaited trial on suspicion of the wilful murder of Rebecca, which she had brought about more than eighteen months before.

Depending on the severity of an accusation, prisoners could spend some considerable time on remand awaiting trial before the Assize Courts, or 'Great Sessions', as these were normally held in York only twice a year during Lent and summer. Judges rode on horseback from one county town to the next, trying all those charged with criminal offences too serious to be dealt with by the magistrates at the Quarter Sessions. At these Assize Courts capital offences were heard – crimes including murder, manslaughter and rape as well as treason, major fraud or theft, arson, riot and rebellion. Guilt on any of these counts carried the death penalty before 1836, the year in which capital punishment was abolished for crimes other than those of murder, attempted murder and, in theory at least, treason.

Mary would have been detained in York's 'Female Prison', which had been built in 1780, next to the Debtor's Prison, in a bid to ease the gaol's overcrowding. At the end of the seventeenth century, it was decided to build a new prison inside the bailey of York Castle and work commenced on the new County Gaol which opened in 1705, having taken four years to build – this building became known as the Debtor's prison but proved inadequate with regards to the increasing prisoner population. The impressive façade of the Female Prison mirrored the architecture of the newly appointed County Court opposite, designed by John Carr and completed three years earlier in 1777. This was where

Mr Justice Simon Le Blanc would preside over Mary's trial during the Lent Assizes which opened on Friday 17 March 1809.

At this point, with Mary's court case pending, we must examine the knowledge and extent of John Bateman's involvement in his wife's criminal activities. Mr Snowden, whose house in Leeds had been left in Mary's care, had happened to see the newspaper article concerning Mary's arrest and had hurried back to Leeds from Bradford to discover that his home had been plundered of just about every item he owned. On the issue of a search warrant, as some of the Snowden's belongings were found in the Bateman's house, along with those of the Perigos, John Bateman was arrested. It is difficult to believe that at no point did he question his wife as to the influx of furniture and goods into their house, clearly not their property. If Mary had indeed bought the items herself, where had she found the money to do so? As his was not a capital offence, John Bateman's case would have been heard at the next Quarter Session, the Leeds charter of incorporation of 1661 having given the Borough the right to hold its own Quarter and Petty Sessions, which were independent of the West Riding courts. As the name suggests, Quarter Sessions were county courts held by magistrates four times a year, dealing with criminal matters from petty theft rising to rape, along with administrative matters such as licensing. Unfortunately, there is a gap in the Order and Indictment Books for Leeds Quarter Sessions for the period 1809–1844. We do know, however, from the account of Mary's trial, that John Bateman was imprisoned pending his own appearance at the next session. The fact that he was acquitted as either principal or accomplice to Mary's crime was thought at the time more on account of his good luck than good conduct, though up to this point, he was considered to have been of irreproachable character, having been in the same employment for sixteen years, noted for the sobriety of his conduct and his 'close application to business, not having lost a single day during the whole of that period, except when he visited friends'. After all, John himself had been practiced upon by his own wife. He could not, surely, have been entirely ignorant of Mary's frauds, as he had collected the bedstead purchased by the Perigos for Miss Blythe from where it was being kept by Mr Sutton, at the Lion & Lamb Inn on Kirkgate, allegedly awaiting collection by the boatman of Miss Blythe's brother. Taking the bedstead to his employer's workshop, and then on to their home in Water Lane, on enquiry, John claimed to have bought the bedstead himself. Though cleared of the charges against him, things did not end well for John Bateman. In spite of all the money that Mary had extorted over the years, she didn't enrich her family; her husband was left in extreme poverty, his debts unpaid, and eventually his house was broken up and his furniture sold. With regard to John Bateman's culpability in the knowledge of the murder, or perhaps we should say *murders* perpetrated by his wife (which in view of Mary's history must be pluralised, even though she was only tried and convicted of the single murder of Rebecca Perigo), we cannot know if he was free from all or any criminal connivance in the acts, only that he was never placed on trial as an accessory.

At this juncture, we must look at the prevalent contemporary chauvinistic attitude to female criminality. Another moralising gem drawn from *The Extraordinary Life*, that as women were 'naturally much more amiable, tender and compassionate than the other sex, [they] become, when they pervert the dictates of nature, more remorseless and cruel, and can conceive and execute the most diabolical of crimes' summed up the feeling of the age. Mary's guilt, and guile, was doubtless viewed as wholly in accord with this universal view, and while criminality held a certain fascination in the nineteenth century, and still does as we shall see in the concluding chapter of this book, murder represents the ultimate appalling act and murders committed by women have always been regarded as more shocking. Since women were regarded as the weaker sex, legally passing all they owned to their husbands with their wedding vows, a situation in which a woman was exposed as a murderer violated their femininity and turned the world upside down. There is a sense in which the law was harsher – and society more outraged – by a female killer than a male. In court, these women were tried as individuals and allowed to give their own testimony.

Even modes of execution personified the inequality of the sexes - a stark example was that while hanging was the standard capital punishment for a husband who murdered his wife, the ultimate inequality was exercised in the sentencing of wives who murdered their husbands, as those found guilty of maricide were executed by strangulation and their bodies then burned at the stake under the old Tudor law of 'petty treason'. The last person to be executed in this way in Yorkshire was Elizabeth Boardingham, her death penalty carried out at York's Tyburn on 20 March 1776.

Chapter 8

The Gates Of Mercy Are Closed

Mary was to be tried at York Crown Court, opposite the Female Prison in which she was held, on Friday 17 March 1809. Charged with the wilful murder of Rebecca Perigo of Bramley in the West Riding, in the month of May, 1807, Mary appeared in the dock of the packed courtroom before the presiding judge, Sir Simon Le Blanc. Wearing scarlet robes lined with ermine and a full-bottomed wig in the seventeenth century style, Le Blanc appeared as the 'face of justice'. While literacy levels were increasing amongst the population, the late eighteenth and early nineteenth centuries were still a visual culture, and the importance of visual symbolism was not lost on the judicial system, with the importance of spectacle evoking awe from 'ordinary men', as asserted by Judge William Blackstone in his *Commentaries* published in 1831, 'the novelty and very parade' of a judge's appearance having 'no small influence on the multitude.' The black cap was placed on a judge's head when he pronounced the death sentence and the royal coat of arms flashed a gilded power on the wall behind him. Le Blanc was a graduate of Trinity Hall, Cambridge and had been called to the Bar of the Inner Temple in 1773. In 1799, he was knighted and appointed as a judge of King's Bench.

As the trial got underway, Mr Williams opened the case for the prosecution. Mr John Hardy, Recorder for the Borough of Leeds, who would later go into politics, then addressed the jury telling them that 'he had to detail circumstances of as extraordinary folly on the one hand, and of iniquity on the other, as ever came before a court of justice.'

And while the event which occasioned the accused's prosecution had taken place nearly two years previously, he would nevertheless be able to show, in evidence, why the case had not been brought sooner – a case he described as ranking 'amongst the most artful and diabolical that ever entered the human imagination'. The jury, whose names we do not know, was made up of 'twelve men and true' who would have been property holders in the Leeds area. In theory at least, they would have no prior connection with the case.

The pivotal aspect of the case was whether or not Mary Bateman had actually supplied the poisonous powders which had killed Rebecca Perigo, and whether she knew them to be poison. Hardy pursued the line that, in defrauding the Perigos, Mary knew that she would not escape detection forever, and had therefore decided to employ poison to avoid exposure and punishment.

If Mary's plans had worked, the 'Miss Blythe' correspondence would have been destroyed and both Perigos would have been found dead in their own home, the victims of a tragic suicide pact to which they had been reduced by poverty. As matters stood, it was 'Providence' that the life of William Perigo had been preserved, and Mary Bateman disclosed as 'an imposter and a cheat'.

Hardy dwelt on the destruction of Miss Blythe's letters, and while in most instances the Perigos had done as they had been instructed, William had committed the contents of those letters burnt to memory, and the two surviving letters that he hadn't consigned to the fire, dated 12 and 28 August 1808 and purporting to have come from Miss Blythe, were proven to be in Mary's hand. Summoned to give evidence in court, the prosecution produced John Bateman's employer, Mr Wright, as a witness, and he confirmed that the letters shown to him were in Mary's handwriting, he having been acquainted with the accused for seventeen years. He may even have seen Mary's earliest written fraud when she had hurried to Wright's premises nearly fifteen years earlier carrying the forged letter with the news that her husband's father was near death, the false pretext which had allowed her to strip and sell the contents of their marital home in John Bateman's absence all those years ago.

The prosecution further alluded to the instruction that if the Perigos were to fall ill as a consequence of taking the powders supplied by Miss Blythe and given them by Mary, they were on no account to seek medical advice. It was also noted that the date in 1807 on which the Perigos were to start using the powders, the 11 May, was also convenient, allowing a comfortable margin before Mary was supposed to have made reparation to the Perigos on behalf of Miss Blythe in the sum of £20. This was to have been on the 20th of that month, by which time she anticipated that the couple would be dead. Hardy drew attention to the instruction in another of Miss Blythe's letters, dated 5 May, urging the Perigos not to let the boy who regularly ate with them eat any of the puddings. Hardy put it to the jury that this may have been compassion on Mary's part, but it was more likely that a child would show the symptoms of poisoning more quickly. This would not only put the Perigos on their guard, it may have put the authorities onto Mary all the sooner. These points, coupled with the direction that the Perigos should start taking the poison-saturated honey if any ill effects did come about, caused Hardy to exclaim 'can any person after this entertain a doubt, that the prisoner at the bar wished their destruction!'

As the trial, which was to last eleven hours proceeded, indictment after damning indictment was presented, from the thorough search made by constables in Scarborough which had revealed, predictably, that no such person as Miss Blythe existed, to the discovery of arsenic pills found in the Bateman's house in Water Lane when the premises were searched after Mary had initially been taken into custody.

Of the witnesses called by the prosecution, Sarah Stead, Rebecca Perigo's niece, was the first to take the stand. It was she who had innocently enough recommended the services of Mary Bateman to her distressed aunt. Her testimony was followed by the examination of William Perigo which occupied upwards of four hours. After the full relation of his and his wife's dealings with Mary Bateman, Judge Le Blanc asked him whether he was certain of 'what he had advanced on these points' to which Perigo replied 'I'll abide by it while I live, and I will abide by it in another world for ever.'

Various other witnesses were called to testify, amongst them Thomas Dobbin, from whom William Perigo had bought Miss Blythe's bed and bedstead, and a William Hick, book-keeper at the Leeds Coach-office who recalled William Perigo bringing in a parcel addressed to 'Miss Blythe, Centre Hotel, Buxton'. He related how, three weeks later, a woman came to the Coach-office to enquire after the parcel; presumably Mary, who must have expected the parcel to have been returned to Leeds as the recipient did not exist. However, an oversight on the part of Hick meant that the return of the parcel was delayed until after Mary's arrest, and when the parcel was finally recovered and the contents investigated, it just so happened to contain the Perigo family Bible, demanded by Miss Blythe the previous October.

Detrimental testimonies continued to issue from the witness stand. Winifred Bond, who was employed by Mary to run various errands, stated that she frequently took letters to post offices in different towns for her. She was a perfect choice on Mary's part, as conveniently Winifred could not read. She had on several occasions taken letters over to Bramley to deliver to the Perigos, and often returned with items such as a brewing tub and some malt, as well as some flour and some tea. She stated that Mary was quite implicit as to what Winifred should say if William Perigo were ever to question her, that she should tell him she was employed by Miss Blythe as a domestic, for her house in Fulneck which at the time had a flourishing Moravian church, about five miles west of the centre of Leeds. In fact, Winifred lived in

Haworth, near Keighley, not yet the home of the Brontes, having been obliged to leave Leeds at Mary's request. When Judge Le Blanc asked the witness how Mary Bateman had 'obliged' her to quit her home in Leeds, Winifred replied that 'she was afraid', fearing the supernatural powers which she supposed Mary to possess.

When Rose Howgate, neighbour to the Perigos and a long-time friend of Rebecca's was called to the witness stand, she told the court how she had visited at 10 o'clock on the morning of the fateful Saturday when the final pudding had been prepared with the last packet of poisonous powder. She'd found the couple well, and Rebecca doing some washing. However, when she returned later that afternoon she found both William and Rebecca very unwell indeed and vomiting, and that 'the colour of what came from them was green and yellow and very frothy', added to which she could hear her neighbours' continuous vomiting from her own home next door. Over the course of the following week, Rose Howgate had continued with her neighbourly ministrations, until Rebecca's death on the Sunday following. Being present when the deceased was laid out, Rose noted that the body 'was covered in every part with black and white spots, but particularly about the neck and stomach'. Rebecca's lips were also 'exceedingly black' and a great quantity of froth issued from the mouth, and her body was 'so offensive that every person about her was under the necessity of smoking'. In the days before the inherent health risks of tobacco were identified, smoking pipes or the taking of snuff was often employed as a way of masking foul smells.

Clearly suspicious of the cause and circumstances surrounding Rebecca's death, it was Rose Howgate and another neighbour, John Rogerson, who had taken upon themselves the idea of experimentally feeding some of the poisoned pudding to a cat. The poor creature died after vomiting yellow and green matter. John Rogerson was also present with a Joshua Stockdale (possibly Rebecca's brother – her maiden name was Stockdale) when William Perigo opened the silk purses that were supposed to have contained the guinea notes and coins, and it was also Joshua Stockdale who had accompanied William Perigo, along with Chief Constable Duffield, to the canal side meeting arranged with Mary Bateman. He verified the conversation that had taken place between them before Mary had been taken into custody.

Further evidence of Mary's procurement of poison was provided by eleven-year-old Thomas Gristy, who remembered that about two years previously he had accompanied Jack Bateman, Mary's son, who would himself have been eleven years old at the time, in April 1807 to Mr Clough's apothecary shop in Kirkgate. At this time the sale of drugs and poisons was practically unrestricted, and they could be bought like any other commodity, arsenic often being employed in pest control. In this instance when Jack Bateman handed over the paper upon which was written the request for 4d worth of arsenic, Mr Clough had refused to sell it to the boys saying that it was poison, even though Jack Bateman maintained it was to be used 'to kill bugs with'.

The most damning witness testimony came however from Thomas Chorley, a practicing surgeon of nearly seventeen years standing from Call Lane in Leeds who was listed in the Leeds Directory of 1798, under the 'Physic' section. It was Chorley who had examined William Perigo on the day after his wife's death, he having fallen ill after eating but a single mouthful of the sixth Saturday pudding and just two teaspoons of the 'special' honey, and had noted symptoms indicative of poisoning in his patient. Chorley had also analysed the contents of the jar of honey from which Rebecca had eaten so freely. His personal observations and the tests he had carried out on the dog were all indicative of poison. He also carried out an analysis of the bottle found in Mary's possession on the day of her arrest, when she had arranged to meet William Perigo at the canal side. The bottle and its content were produced in court, and the solution confirmed as a spirituous liquid, probably rum, but also containing two powders, the lighter of which it was supposed was oatmeal while the other was arsenic.

In addition to the testimony provided by Chorley, two further expert witnesses from the medical fraternity were called to the stand and examined regarding the symptoms Rebecca had suffered before and at her death. Dr Lawson of York and Mr James Lucas, formerly a consulting surgeon of Leeds but at the time of Mary's trial practising in Masham, both concurred, in their opinion, that from the evidence they had heard Rebecca Perigo's death could not have arisen from any 'natural disease' and that her symptoms 'were such as would be produced by corrosive sublimate of mercury being received into the stomach'. It would appear that Mary had covered her bases and had employed two different poisons – sublimate of mercury in the 'special' honey (which Chorley had identified), and arsenic to lace the pudding powders.

At this juncture, the verdict seemed a foregone conclusion; Mary had no counsel, and no recourse to explain or contradict the evidence presented with any satisfactory testimony of her own, other than that taken down in her examination by the Leeds magistrate subsequent to her arrest and now read before the court.

The lop-sided, not to say unfair, nature of the judicial system in 1809 is exposed by this. Justice was supposed to be blind and impartial, its scales weighed by evidence. Despite the acquisition of considerable sums of money over the years from various scams, Mary could probably not afford a lawyer. Given the prosecution's evidence and the witnesses called, he would have had his work cut out to sway a jury, but stranger things have happened. Let us for a moment assume that Mary *did* have counsel. What could he have done?

Initially, he would have denied all charges on Mary's behalf and would have cross-examined the prosecution witnesses. He would have challenged Wright's assertion that the Miss Blythe letters were in Mary's handwriting. Wright was not a graphology expert and there is still huge controversy about what handwriting can tell us forensically. The barrister would then have called into question the competence of the Scarborough police who had been unable to find Miss Blythe. There was no doubt that, had the woman been genuine, her psychic powers would have made her reclusive and not the sort to be listed in the town's Directories. He may also have put a doubt into the jury's minds about the Leeds police search of the Batemans' house which had produced the arsenic pills. We have already established that arsenic had conventional household uses at the time and that is before any assertion, later commonplace, of the police planting evidence to bolster their case.

Sarah Stead offered nothing incriminating other than that she had introduced Mary to her aunt so a defence counsel might have let her get off lightly. William Perigo would have spent far longer than his four hours in the witness box. A good brief would have had every sympathy for the man's loss, so that he should not alienate the jury, but would point out that for most of Miss Blythe's correspondence, the court only had William's memory and this was not sufficient. Even the prosecution had alluded to 'an extraordinary folly' on Perigo's part and a clever defence lawyer could have pushed this to the point where the man appeared an imbecile whose testimony could not be relied upon.

The calling of Thomas Dobbin as a witness would merely have served to prove Perigo's stupidity. The man had bought a bed from him, which takes us nowhere near the assumption of murder. In the case of William Hick, the book-keeper at the Leeds Coach-office, if Mary was the woman who had called to collect a parcel addressed to Miss Blythe, why didn't he point her out in court? Winifred Bond's testimony could easily have been demolished. She was illiterate and afraid of Mary. On either score, defence counsel could have called into question her reliability.

Rose Howgate's testimony did not point to Mary at all. She had seen the pudding preparation and witnessed the poison's effects, but Mary, of course, was nowhere to be seen. The defence would have pointed this out too. Little Thomas Gristy was almost irrelevant. It is likely that children's testimony was not taken as seriously as adults' in the courts of the day and all the boy had done was to witness Mary's son trying to buy arsenic, ostensibly for legal reasons – 'to kill bugs with'. Circumstantial evidence like this has hanged people but it has acquitted them too.

The defence counsel would probably have had most difficulty with Mr Chorley, the surgeon, but he would have found an expert witness of his own who would have rebutted Chorley's findings. The later infamous poisoning cases of the century – Charles Bravo, James Maybrick, the many victims of William Palmer – all produced rebuttal witnesses of this type. All of the science would, in all probability, have gone straight over the heads of the jury, so the issue would have come down to personalities – both of the duelling doctors and the clashing counsel.

As it was, there was no defence counsel. Under the law as it stood, Mary was not allowed to speak in her own defence so the arraignment testimony had to suffice. It said that it had been more than three years since she had been in Leeds, variously residing in Manchester, Bedale, Richmond and Masham, and that she had not been in Leeds when William Perigo claimed he had been instructed to bring her the half a peck of wheat, amongst various items extorted from the Perigos at the behest of Miss Blythe. She herself had contributed half the money toward the purchase of the cheese, presumably the six to eight pound one requested in Miss Blythe's letter of October 1806, and that 'she never had any honey or powders' and that Rebecca Perigo 'never brought any honey pot to her'. She had never spoken to either husband or wife about any honey, and neither her husband nor anyone 'never fetched any powder'. In short her defence was a straightforward denial of any involvement in the death of Rebecca, Mary insisting that it was 'utterly false' that she 'ever did send for any poison by any person'. Any avenue of opportunity in shifting the blame to Miss Blythe had already been closed off of course when the constables in Scarborough had failed to find any such person. In fact, Mary had already admitted to the Leeds magistrates that there was in fact no such person as Miss Blythe in existence. Indeed, during her arraignment at Leeds, Mary had also stated 'that all the letters were written by Hannah Potts except the last five or six'. Whether Hannah Potts really existed, perhaps as an acquaintance of Mary's, or was merely another invention on her part like Miss Blythe, we will never know.

In his summing up of the case, Sir Simon Le Blanc reminded the jury that to bring in a guilty verdict they had to satisfy themselves on three points. These were that Rebecca Perigo had died from poisoning, that the poison had been administered with the knowledge and contrivance of Mary Bateman, and that it had been done in the expectation of causing Rebecca Perigo's death. The jury, as was always the case in those days, was entirely male and the judge went on to remind them to render an impartial verdict and that although there was a strong case against Mary for having systematically defrauded the Perigos, this did not automatically make her guilty of murder. However, in view of the overwhelming evidence presented by the prosecution, after conferring for a very short time, the jury returned a verdict of guilty. Accordingly Judge Le Blanc placed the black cloth sentencing cap over his powdered wig and proceeded to pass sentence of death:

> 'Mary Bateman, you have been convicted of wilful murder by a jury who, after having examined your case with caution, have,

constrained by the force of evidence, pronounced you guilty. It only remains for me to fulfil my painful duty by passing upon you the awful sentence of the law. After you have been so long in the situation in which you now stand, and harassed as your mind must be by the long detail of your crimes and by listening to the sufferings you have occasioned, I do not wish to add to your distress by saying more than my duty renders necessary. Of your guilt, there cannot remain a particle of doubt in the breast of anyone who has heard your case. You entered into a long and premeditated system of fraud, which you carried on for a length of time which is most astonishing, and by means which one would have supposed could not, in this age and nation, have been practised with success. To prevent a discovery of your complicated fraud, and the punishment which must have resulted therefrom, you deliberately contrived the death of the persons you had so grossly injured, and that by means of poison, a mode of destruction against which there is no sure protection. But your guilty design was not fully accomplished, and, after so extraordinary a lapse of time, you are reserved as a signal example of the justice of that mysterious Providence, which, sooner or later, overtakes guilt like yours. At the very time when you were apprehended, there is the greatest reason to suppose, that if your surviving victim had met you alone, as you wished him to do, you would have administered to him a more deadly dose, which would have completed the diabolical project you had long before formed, but which at that time only partially succeeded; for upon your person, at that moment, was found a phial containing a most deadly poison. For crimes like yours, in this world, the gates of mercy are closed. You afforded your victim no time for preparation, but the law, while it dooms you to death, has, in its mercy, afforded you time for repentance, and the assistance of

> pious and devout men, whose admonitions, and prayers, and counsels may assist to prepare you for another world, where even your crimes, if sincerely repented of, may find mercy.
>
> 'The sentence of the law is, and the court doth award it, that you be taken to the place from whence you came, and from thence, on Monday next, to the place of execution, there to be hanged by the neck until you are dead, and that your body be given to the surgeons to be dissected and anatomized. And may Almighty God have mercy upon your soul.'

With regard to the stipulation of Mary's sentence concerning 'dissection', in 1752 the 'Act for the better preventing the horrid Crime of Murder', more commonly known as the 'Murder Act', mandated the dissection of the bodies of executed murderers (including females), though the gibbeting of the remains of male malefactors was still reserved for those found guilty of particularly heinous or high profile crimes.

Dissection was viewed with a very real horror. A practice formerly prohibited by the Catholic Church, after the English Reformation of the sixteenth century, as medical research grew so did the need for cadavers. By the 1700s, in England, the bodies of executed criminals and the 'unclaimed poor' were given over to feed the need of surgical teaching schools and hospitals. The legal supply of corpses for anatomical purposes did not provide enough 'subjects' and eventually the demand for cadavers for medical use outstripped the supply – in 1812 there were twenty-six Medical Schools in Great Windmill Street, London, alone. Body snatching, the gruesome trade of the Resurrection Men, became a lucrative sphere of criminal activity in itself. Certainly the sentence of dissection increased the deterrent effect of the death penalty by preying on the very real dread felt by most of the population at the thought of dismemberment after death.

The prevalent and strong belief that dissection and the desecration of a deceased body, rendering it incomplete, would prevent an individual's entry into Heaven is not as archaic as it would seem.

When body snatching reached its zenith, with the Resurrection Men working overtime to exhume the bodies of the recently dead, it was not unusual for relatives and friends of someone who had just died to watch over the body until burial, and then to keep watch over the grave after interment, to stop it being removed and violated. Iron coffins, too, were used frequently, or the graves were protected by a framework of iron bars called *mortsafes*. Watchtowers were even built within some cemeteries and night watchman employed to deter those intent on their gory trade. Indeed, in some cases the public feeling against the practice was so strong that bodies were frequently 'saved' from the surgeon's table by the surge of angry crowds intent on snatching the body away post execution, ensuring an intact Christian burial. One notable case in point was the cadaver of celebrity criminal Dick Turpin, executed on York's Knavesmire gallows in 1739 before a vast crowd, appreciative of his final bravado in the shadow of the noose. In spite of being buried in a very deep grave in the churchyard of St George's, Turpin's body was later found disinterred and in the garden of one of the city surgeons. However, the dissectionists were thwarted, as after keeping Turpin's body in the Blue Boar Inn overnight (in those days a public house often had a room that was used as a temporary mortuary), to prevent any further 'body snatching' attempts Turpin was re-buried in St George's Churchyard, this time the coffin was filled with unslaked quicklime.

The first to suffer the post-mortem fate of dissection after the 'Murder Act' came into force on 1 June 1752 was seventeen-year-old Thomas Wilford. Found guilty of the murder of his wife, who Wilford had stabbed to death just one week after their wedding, he was executed on 22 of June 1752, hanged upon London's infamous 'Tyburn Tree', the site of which is today occupied by Marble Arch.

In the case of Mary Bateman, execution was scheduled for the Monday following the trial. It was usual for all those prisoners condemned at the previous Assizes to await the next scheduled day of execution and then be hanged in groups, irrespective of gender. In York, Monday was the designated day for murderers to be hanged, while the execution of other criminals was kept back for Saturdays as this allowed for the largest weekend crowds.

Yet she still had one last trick up her sleeve. When the Clerk of the Arraigns asked 'Mary Bateman, what have you to say, why immediate execution should not be awarded against you?' Mary burst into floods of tears, and announced to the court that she was twenty-two weeks pregnant.

Chapter 9

'Quick' with Child?

Under English common law 'pleading the belly' permitted women in the later stages of pregnancy to be reprieved of their death sentences until after the delivery of the child. The plea did not constitute a defence and could only be made after a guilty verdict had been passed, and verification of the claimant's condition was determined by what was termed as a 'jury of matrons', customarily drawn from the women observing the proceedings in the courtroom. If found to be 'quick with child' (that is, the movements of the foetus could be detected), a reprieve would be granted until after the birth of the child, after which the sentence of execution was reinstated and enacted on the date set for the next round of hangings.

Some fortunate women awarded such a reprieve would even subsequently be granted pardons, or have their sentences commuted to transportation or imprisonment. In spite of the perceived increase in levels of crime, the late eighteenth century witnessed the development of non-capital punishments such as transportation and imprisonment as an alternative sentence for certain crimes. Needless to say, consequently the system was open to abuse. In Daniel Defoe's novel *Moll Flanders* written in 1721, one character successfully pleads her belly despite being 'no more with child than the judge that tried [her]'. And the practice of selecting a jury of matrons from the courtroom observers opened up the opportunity for planting sympathetic accomplices in the public gallery, causing one eighteenth century commentator to complain that female felons would have 'Matrons of [their] own Profession ready at hand, who, right or wrong, bring their wicked Companions quick with Child to the great Impediment of Justicc.'

While of course such examinations could not have detected the condition of those who had only recently conceived, in theory, the very early stages of pregnancy, prior to the foetus 'quickening', did not qualify for a stay of execution. There had been an earlier example of this in the execution of Christian Murphy on 18 March 1789 at Newgate for counterfeiting silver coins. Though she had 'pleaded her belly', the matrons who examined her concluded that she was '... not quick with child, but it was their opinion that she was with child, and has been so a short time'. Her execution went ahead nevertheless, and Christian Murphy was the last woman in England to be strangled and burned at the stake, the crime of 'coining' classed as petty treason.

In an attempt to limit the abuse of the system further, the law decreed that no woman could be granted a second reprieve on an original sentence passed if she were later found to be with child, even if they were actually pregnant. While the gaoler or local sheriff in charge of any female prisoner falling pregnant while held in their custody was subject to a fine, this threat did not always present an effective deterrent however, as the case of Mary Burgan shows. Originally convicted in 1705 of killing her first baby, for which she would ordinarily have been hanged, while awaiting trial at York, Burgan became pregnant again, in all probability by the Turnkey, Thomas Ward. Mary was allowed to live in the prison with her son Thomas, who grew up in York Castle Gaol, supported by payments made by the Three Ridings until 1718 when he was put out to apprenticeship at the age of 12. Mary had been listed as a reprieve in the Calendar of Felons for York Castle 1707, and her sentence subsequently commuted to that of transportation, but it appears that she was eventually released under a general pardon issued by Queen Anne in 1710, the power of pardon being a royal prerogative of mercy in the gift of the monarch of the United Kingdom and most frequently cited in cases where the death penalty had been given. As for Turnkey Ward, clearly not all the criminals were behind bars! Responsible for the daily running of the gaol, Ward exploited his position, charging a fee for showing visitors round the cells. He was a bully and an extortionist and forced prisoners to buy food and drink from him at inflated prices. Matters came to a head in 1709 when prisoners signed a petition against his 'inhumane and unchristian' behaviour. Nevertheless, in 1718 Ward became the Governor of York Castle Gaol.

Other women who claimed to be *enceinte* – with child – were also fortunate enough to escape the noose, though punishment for their crimes was not entirely negated. Both Elizabeth Cahill and Naomi Hollings were transported for a sentence of fourteen years apiece after both had given birth in York Castle Gaol.

Elizabeth Cahill had indulged in a spot of pick pocketing in Leeds Market on New Year's Eve 1728. After languishing in gaol for some time, she was reprieved on successfully pleading her belly and her daughter, Ann, was baptised in York Castle on 15 May 1733. Elizabeth's sentence was revised and she was sentenced to transportation, enacted in the summer of 1735.

Naomi Hollings had been sentenced to death at the Lent Assizes of 1739 for the theft of money and goods after breaking and entering a private dwelling house. Again she was reprieved on successfully pleading her belly, and on 13 June 1739 her son was christened 'Castellus' in York Castle, an apt name given the child's place of birth. Her sentence was also reinstated after the birth, though again commuted to that of transportation the following summer of 1740.

Not every convicted female felon fared so well however. Despite legitimately pleading her belly, Elizabeth Webster had her sentence reinstated for the poisoning of her husband and was ultimately executed on 5 March 1744 some five months after the baptism of her son in York

Castle Gaol. There is no record as to what became of the orphaned William Webster, but a prison birth in the eighteenth century was in all probability not the most auspicious of beginnings for a child. Some were lucky enough to receive support for their upkeep from the Three Ridings until old enough to be put out to an apprenticeship, usually around 12 years of age, as was the case with Turnkey Ward's progeny.

What was the outcome in Mary's case? To verify her plea, Judge Le Blanc ordered the sheriff to empanel a jury of matrons from the courtroom, twelve married women who would be asked to ascertain whether or not Mary was indeed pregnant. This order 'created a general consternation among the ladies, who hastened to quit the court, to prevent the execution of so painful an office being imposed upon them', but, anticipating this reaction, the judge ordered the doors of the courtroom be locked, lest the jury of empanelled matrons try to escape their duty. In about half-an-hour, twelve married women had been sworn in and charged to inquire 'whether the prisoner was quick with child?' Mary was escorted to another room where, after intimate examination, the twelve women eventually pronounced that her claim was unfounded. Even if Mary's plea had been verified, it is unlikely that in view of the high profile of her case she would have been granted any reprieve other than that of delaying the inevitable. Mary was remanded back to prison. Pregnant or not, the records of Mary's last days in prison confirm that she was allowed to have her youngest child with her in the condemned cell until her removal for execution.

At the time it was common practice for a woman's children to accompany their mother to prison, especially in the case of infants classed as care-dependent of a nursing mother. Such children often remained in the cell with their mothers until they were executed, clinging on for dear life as their parent was led away to the gallows. While the sex of the child that shared Mary's cell is not stipulated, in all likelihood it was her son James Bateman who was incarcerated along with his mother, the parish records of St Peter's, Leeds showing his date of baptism as 19 July 1807. After her trial, it was noted that as soon as Mary was returned to her cell she 'took her infant child and gave it breast', a circumstance which 'considerably affected the gaoler who attended her on this melancholy occasion'.

Over the course of the intervening weekend, between her receiving sentence of death and her appointed execution, the Ordinary, or prison chaplain, the Reverend George Brown, was at great pains to prevail on Mary that she acknowledge and confess to her crimes before her date with the gallows. Had it been forthcoming, as well as assuaging the threat to her mortal soul, Mary's confession would have provided legitimacy to the court's decision, and justification for her hanging, as well as material for sensationalised public consumption, as such confessions were often published and devoured by a populace hungry for the sorrowful repentances of those who had formerly pleaded their innocence. Exemplified by the popularity of 'broadsheets', these confessions were published as public accounts, and in turn proved a significant contribution to bolstering the legitimacy of the justice system. Mary's refusal to make any admission of her guilt was the exception rather than the rule however, as the majority of convicted murderers, regardless of gender, played their role in the propagation of 'public justice' by admitting to the horror of their crimes after condemnation, 'acquiescing to the justness of their fates'. Nevertheless, Mary held fast. At the Reverend Brown's mention of the deaths of the Quaker Kitchin sisters and their mother back in September 1803, Mary said she would not be pressed on the subject as at the time she had been 'confined in childbirth'. Using the baptismal records of St Peter's Church from 1804, Mary can only have been in the very early stages of pregnancy, if, indeed, she was pregnant at the time at all.

In spite of her circumstances, observers noted that Mary continued to behave in a decorous manner; she joined in with the 'customary offices of devotion' but she showed no sign of remorse or repentance, and 'maintained her caution and mystery to the last'.

On Sunday, the day before her execution, Mary wrote a letter to her husband, who had not visited his wife since the guilty verdict had been pronounced. With this letter, she enclosed her wedding ring and asked him to give it to their daughter. While she lamented the disgrace she had brought upon John and the family, and admitted to being guilty of *some frauds* [my italics], she nevertheless maintained her innocence and continued to deny her involvement in Rebecca Perigo's death. Mary also wrote in the letter that she had made her peace with God. As this was Mary's last letter, and the only one in her own words, the transcription in full, as it appeared in Rede's *York Castle in the Nineteenth Century* is perhaps warranted:

> 'My Dear Husband,
>
> I do send you herewith my ring, that as I had of you when I was mor[e] happy, and had not disgraced you. You must give it to my dear girl, who will keep it for ever in remembrance of her poor unhappy mother. Though you are disgraced by me, I trust in Christ you will forgive me, as I am sorry and hope to be forgiven. I am innocent of murder - I did get the money at many times, but that was all. I did never destroy that woman, for whom I am to suffer - I am innocent of that, though I did many things else for which I am much aggrieved. I have made my peace with my God, and am easy in mind. The worst is when I will part with my blessed baby - God bless you; forgive your poor wife who is only in affliction for you. To-morrow will end all here, and the Lord will care for me hereafter.
>
> Your loving and sorrowful wife,
>
> MARY BATEMAN.'

Yet in spite of her outward show of contrition, it was later reported by the *Leeds Intelligencer* newspaper that Mary continued her criminal habits, even from the condemned cell, telling the fortune of one of her female attendants for the price of a guinea, and incredibly, even during her final few hours, Mary found time to commit one last fraud – perhaps resigned to her fate, she thought she had nothing to lose. With her usual cunning, she convinced a fellow prisoner that if she could somehow get hold of a specified sum of money, by allowing Mary to stitch the coins into her stays (the contemporary term for a corset) this 'charm' would somehow bring her sweetheart to visit her in prison. But when the lover's promised visit failed to materialise, the girl tore open her bodice and discovered that the coins had mysteriously vanished. Mary protested her innocence to the accusation of this theft with the same conviction she had applied to her denial of her having any part in the death of Rebecca Perigo.

The Reverend Brown again visited Mary on Sunday evening, but in spite of his exhortations to confess to her sins on the eve of her execution, Mary resolutely maintained her denial of the crime for which she was to be hanged the following morning.

At 5am on Monday 20 March, Mary was woken and removed from her cell to attend communion service in the prison chapel, and while this afforded her a further opportunity to unburden herself with a confession, no admissions were forthcoming. Mary kissed her youngest child, still asleep on the bed in the condemned cell, for the last time before being led away to the gallows, the preparations of which must have been clearly audible. The scaffold was almost certainly permanently erected, but the ropes had to be tried and tested and this was not a silent operation. It must have been an eerie experience for those shortly to die as they heard the crash of the drop and the creak of the rope.

Mary was to be hanged on York's New Drop, the executions formerly carried out on the Knavesmire upon the 'York Tyburn', or 'Three Legged Mare' as it was known, having ceased in 1801. The former gallows, which overlooked the racecourse, had been a cleverly designed tripod arrangement that in name and structure echoed its London counterpart, the Tyburn Tree, a triple gallows configuration allowing multiple hangings on the same day.

Although the public spectacle of execution was supposed to act as a deterrent to the populace, making them afraid and fearful of falling victim to the same fate, this was not always the case, and amongst those laughing and joking about the awful sight they were about to witness there would inevitably be pickpockets and robbers exploiting the opportunity to work the crowd, literally in the shadow of the gallows. To quote Dr Johnson's opinion of public execution: 'If they do not draw spectators, they do not answer their purpose'; but he had clearly missed the point.

Public hangings often took on a mass entertainment quality, perhaps akin to an open-air concert atmosphere today. Human nature being what it is, these events turned out to be a perversely enjoyable distraction from the routine grind of everyday life. With food and drink on sale, and souvenirs being hawked, crowds including families with young children would bring along a picnic and make a day of it, and despite the obvious taste and enthusiasm for the spectacle of a public execution, the ultimate decision to move the proceedings to York Castle Gaol was heavily influenced by the objectionable initial impression of the City given by the Knavesmire gallows, located as they were next to one of the main highways into York. On execution days, the sight of the gallows were also a cause of major road congestion, a parallel perhaps to the traffic jams resulting from the ghoulish curiosity at the site of an accident today, the gathering crowd impeding traffic flow. In an article printed on 25 July 1800, the *York Herald* explained:

> 'Thus will be removed from one of the principal roads leading to the city that disagreeable nuisance, the gallows; and thus will the inhabitants and passengers be no longer interrupted, and their humanity hurt, by the leading of unfortunate people to the place of execution.'

As a consequence, in order that the 'entrance to the town should no longer be annoyed by dragging criminals through the streets' at a civic meeting it was decided that investment in a new gallows should be made, the cost of which totalled £10 15 shillings. The New Drop, as it became known, constructed by Joseph Halfpenny, joiner of Blake Street in the city, was set up at the back of the Castle in an area bounded by the Castle Mills Bridge and the river Ouse, roughly where the roundabout by St George's car park is today. Looking toward York Castle Museum, still discernable in the wall to the right is a small doorway through which the condemned prisoners were led, a far shorter and less disruptive route than the one formerly taken in an open cart, the condemned sitting on their coffin and already wearing their shroud, jolted on out through Micklegate Bar towards the Knavesmire for their execution. Though sensibility had won the day, the first execution on the New Drop having taken place in 1802, the Knavesmire gallows stood, albeit unused, for a further ten years before being finally dismantled in 1812.

We can only speculate as to why the execution of certain criminals drew more of a crowd than others. Sometimes the notoriety of the crime committed affected the draw (Dick Turpin is a case in point), or even the weather might limit numbers. Special note was always made of any execution where the strength of the crowd was considered to be great, usually referred to in the records as 'a large concourse of spectators' sometimes even resulting in injury to the assembled onlookers. In 1649 the hanging at York of a convicted husband and wife, George and Maria Merrington, proved so great an attraction that the day ended with broken bones. In Mary's case, the crowd was variously estimated to be between five and twenty thousand.

She was not alone on the gallows that Monday morning, as she was hanged in company with a fellow poisoner, Joseph Brown, an agricultural labourer also convicted at the 1809 Lent assizes for the murder of his 55-year-old landlady, Elizabeth Fletcher of Hensal near Ferrybridge, and the attempted murder of her sister Sarah, in 1804. Though suspected at the time of Elizabeth Fletcher's death, Brown escaped justice as there was insufficient proof that he had liberally laced the Fletcher sisters' sweetened ale with an overdose of laudanum. Brown, like Mary, was also widely regarded as possessing some mystical powers, the basis of which was his ability to predict the death of others. Whether or not he foretold his own demise, he was certainly the cause of it, as having later been convicted of theft and sentenced to transportation, while awaiting embarkation for Botany Bay, he confessed to his earlier crimes, the surviving Fletcher sister giving damning evidence against him at his re-trial.

Officiating on the gallows on the morning of the 20th was York's most infamous hangman – the twice-sentenced, twice-reprieved William 'Mutton' Curry. In York, the position of hangman was usually filled by a convicted felon who had been pardoned sentence of death on the condition that he accept the job; some of whom even took on something of a dubious 'celebrity' status. A convicted sheep-stealer, hence his ovine nickname, 'Mutton' Curry was originally a labourer from Thirsk. His sentence of death had been twice commuted to transportation, and while being held in York Castle Gaol in 1802 awaiting his enforced passage to Australia, he was prevailed upon to accept the vacant position of hangman. Curry was known to be partial to a drop of gin, perhaps hardly surprising given the nature of his work, and this consequently led to some less than professional executions. On one occasion, Curry was so drunk *The Times* reported that:

> 'The executioner, in a bungling manner and with great difficulty (being in a state of intoxication), placed the cap over the culprit's face and attempted several times to place the rope round his neck, but was unable.'

It took the assistance of the gaoler and the sheriff's officers to complete the job, before an incensed and increasingly hostile crowd angrily demanding Curry's own execution. On another occasion, clearly the worse for drink, Curry actually ended up falling through the trap door himself. He would go on to hang fourteen Luddites (machine wreckers) on one day in January 1813 and did not actually retire until 1835.

As the time for execution approached, both prisoners proceeded to the gallows, accompanied by the sheriff and his attendants. It was noted that 'the number of persons assembled was much greater than usual for such occasions', many of those turning out to see Mary swing having come a great distance to witness the spectacle, and a large number travelling from Leeds on foot, straggling along the course of today's A64 still linking Leeds to York. One wonders how many of their number were made up of those once swindled by 'The Yorkshire Witch'. Nevertheless, the appearance of Mary upon the gallows 'created a visible emotion among the spectators – not of brutal insult, as once disgraced the British character in the metropolis, but of awe and deep commiseration'. A hushed and respectful silence fell over the assembled crowd during the few moments the prisoners spent in prayer, only interrupted by a half-suppressed cry for 'mercy'. The Reverend Brown made one last attempt at persuading Mary to relieve her conscience and unburden her soul before the drop fell, enquiring whether she had any communication to make? Mary said she was innocent.

It was reported that some of the spectators gathered that morning really thought that Mary would save herself from death at the last moment by employing her supernatural powers to vanish into thin air as the noose tightened – but when the drop fell Mary's life ended, along with that of Joseph Brown, both sent to face 'another more awful tribunal' in the Great Hereafter.

After execution by hanging, it was usual for the body to be left dangling for about half an hour before being cut down and, ordinarily, claimed by friends or relatives for burial. A skilled hangman's knot would ensure the certainty of a broken neck, usually at the third vertebra below the skull, and therefore a swift end, but the alternative was a slow and agonising death by strangulation – the sinister origin of the phrase 'to pull one's leg' and the expression 'hangers on' harking back to the time when a criminal's family would pay someone to pull down on them during their hanging, and thereby minimise their suffering. However, that part of Mary's sentence stipulating 'that your body be given to the surgeons to be dissected and anatomized' was now carried out. Mary Bateman's body was loaded onto a horse-drawn cart to be taken to the Leeds General Infirmary. Yet with the road from York to Leeds thronged with horses and gigs, and those who had come on foot to see the execution, it was close on midnight before the hearse reached its destination. Even at this late hour it was met by 'immense crowds of persons' curious to view Mary's lifeless body. Such was the macabre demand for a look at the deceased murderess that on the following day Mary's corpse was exhibited in the surgeon's room at the infirmary, with threepence admission charged for the privilege. Incredibly the number of people willing to pay exceeded two and a half thousand, many of them touching the body before they left the room, a superstitious precaution against the belief that Mary might interfere with their dreams. Consequently, the sum of £30 was raised for the benefit of the General Infirmary; at least Mary had performed one genuinely charitable deed, even if it were from beyond the grave, though of course she was never actually buried.

Mary's dissection was an 'event' doubtless attended by some who were not aspiring physicians - during the nineteenth century, the spectacle of dissection was quite available to members of the public; they might be patrons, artists, or even ticket-buying curiosity seekers who had paid a high price, certainly in this instance. What is surprising is that Madame Tussaud does not seem to have been interested in capturing Mary's likeness in wax for her 'separate room' as the Chamber of Horrors was then known. It may be that she missed the boat, quite literally, because her touring show was in Dublin during the trial and she moved it to Belfast in May. Pauline Chapman in *Madame Tussaud's Chamber of Horrors* gets Mary's name wrong (calling her Mary Bates) and offers no explanation as to why she was not included in the list of ghoulish exhibits. It would be another twelve years before there were any new additions. After the dissection was complete, the greater part of Mary's skin was removed and tanned and preserved, and strips of the resulting 'leather' sold as lucky charms and curios. To modern eyes, though this undoubtedly appears to have been a grisly practice, and Mary Bateman seemingly one of the earliest murderers to have her skin thus preserved, she was certainly not the last. The skin of William Burke, the murderer of Daft Jamie in the Netherbow district of Edinburgh and the skin of William Corder, who killed Maria Marten in the Red Barn, both appeared in later years as book covers and calling card cases. Mary Bateman's skin 'tanned and distributed in small pieces to different applicants' according to the January 1873 edition of *Notes and Queries* ended up spread all over Yorkshire. Among those who possessed such a gruesome keepsake was William Elmhirst, a Deputy Lieutenant for the West Riding, and though it seems improbable that a man in so upright a position and renowned for his eminently dull character would relish a portion of a murderess, he was a friend of Mr Chorley's, one of the officiating surgeons at the Leeds Infirmary, and the same surgeon who had looked after William Perrigo, and who had provided the analysis of Mary's poisons at her trial. Indeed a folding cup made of Mary's skin certainly belonged to Elmhirst's son Robert at one time. The gruesome fascination didn't end there however, as other portions of Mary's skin were employed to cover books – the Prince of Wales, the future George IV, allegedly owned a volume bound in her skin, shelved in his library at Marlborough House, and other similarly bound tomes were once held in the library of Methley Hall in Yorkshire, though since the house was demolished in 1963, their whereabouts are now unknown.

With regards to the fate of the rest of Mary's mortal remains, amongst the 1867 catalogue of curiosities listed in 'Mr Stubbs' Private Museum' in Ripon, North Yorkshire, appears an entry for 'Part of the Tongue of Mary Bateman, the notorious Yorkshire Witch'. Obviously the macabre memento had later passed into another's hands as in 1891 the editor of *Yorkshire Notes and Queries* wrote that:

> 'The tongue of Mary Bateman is in the possession of a gentleman in Ilkley, with whom we are personally acquainted. There is absolutely no doubt as to its genuineness. The curious reader may see it at any time by the courtesy of the present owner.'

In fact, Mary's pickled tongue was still on a list of those items held by Bolling Hall Museum in Bradford in the 1950s. However, as the exhibit was deemed to be too macabre to be held in the Museum's collection it was destroyed by incineration.

As for Mary's skeleton, this was used initially for anatomy classes and afterwards, together with a plaster cast death mask of her face, put on display in the Leeds Medical School. Here the dismembered skeleton remained for nearly 200 years, before being loaned to the Thackray

Medical Museum in Leeds, along with the death mask where, minus the legs and without the mandible, but bizarrely with an apparent additional rib, it was an exhibit which until very recently could still be viewed by the public. There is perhaps an echo here of Lord Justice-Clerk Boyle officiating at William Burke's trial in December 1829 summing up his sentencing with the words 'And I trust, that if it is ever customary to preserve skeletons, yours will be preserved, in order that posterity may keep in remembrance of your atrocious crimes.' It was and is still on display in the Anatomy Museum of Edinburgh Medical School.

A further tangible vestige of Mary Bateman's execution is also still in existence, held in the archives of the York Museum Trust. This is an original copy of one of the many broadsheets printed to be hawked to the crowds attending that day, detailing the crimes of Mary Bateman and Joseph Brown.

Just like the programmes sold at sporting events today, these single large sheets of paper, printed on one side only, were customarily sold to the audiences that gathered to witness public executions in eighteenth and nineteenth-century Britain as a memento or souvenir of the day's proceedings. Vendors would set up their carts and booths hours before the appointed execution time, selling food, drink, souvenirs and even pornographic material in addition to these broadsheets to a pressing crowd eagerly awaiting the coming judicial spectacle. Ephemeral in nature, these publications were aimed at the middle or lower classes, and most sold for a penny or less and documented the gruesome and gory facts and rumours which surrounded the crimes of those about to be publicly executed. Usually sold near the gallows on the day of the hanging, a woodcut illustration invariably accompanied a description of the final hours of the condemned and their last dying confession, all in sensational, dramatic detail. Even if only a limited number of people witnessed an execution – which was certainly not the case in

York on Monday 20 March 1809 – such pamphlet-style accounts were designed to reach a wider audience.

In this instance measuring a little over fifteen inches long by nine inches wide, the Bateman/Brown broadsheet was produced in William Storry's printshop in Low Petergate in the city. Storry's business was still listed in the second volume of the *History, Directory & Gazetteer of Yorkshire* for 1823, the printing works at number 53 part of a site which had been used as a printing works since before 1768, and an adjacent house, at number 7 Grape Lane having been acquired in 1819 by William Storry as an extension to the works, so clearly Storry was still in business over a decade after Mary's execution, though her eventual legacy would prove to be far more enduring.

Chapter 10

'Damn her name to everlasting fame'

Certainly Mary Bateman achieved a sort of celebrity through the notoriety of her criminal behaviour that still fascinates today. The astonishing nerve of the woman in carrying out her cons and frauds, her ingenuity and her total amorality – she never met a lie she didn't like – have assured her an established place in the list of female murderers and even given the 'Yorkshire Witch' a kind of immortality.

Mary was an 'ordinary' woman turned into an 'extraordinary' one, and in this respect has the 'fame game' really changed? Though today's media coverage facilitates the mass devouring of crime stories and while we may recoil in shock and horror, inherently we wonder why people kill and we are intrigued by the ways in which the deed is accomplished, and with such obvious relish that it seems a part of the ordinary human condition, and ever was it thus. To quote the renowned crime novelist Dorothy L Sayers, 'Death seems to provide the minds of the Anglo-Saxon race with a greater fund of innocent enjoyment than any other single subject.' And the public always has had an appetite for a great villain, especially a female villain. Hogarth's portrayal of Sarah Malcolm, the multiple murderess sketched by the talented satirical, and at times subversive artist in 1733, while she awaited execution in Newgate Gaol, is a perfect case in point. Prints of her portrait were sold at sixpence each, and devoured by an eager public, hungry to put a face to the infamous murderess, much in the same way as *The Extraordinary Life,* published in 1811, two years after Mary Bateman's execution, and running to a twelfth edition. Sensational stories of female criminals figured large in the salacious public imaginations of their time, augmented by the awfulness of their crimes – Sarah Malcolm was charged with the brutal murders of 80-year-old Lydia Duncomb, 60-year-old Elizabeth Harrison, and 17-year-old Ann Price. The two older women had been strangled; Price's throat had been slit. Like Mary Bateman, Sarah Malcolm was to maintain her innocence to the end. Coincidentally, echoing Mary's ultimate fate, though some contemporary accounts report that Sarah was buried, Hogarth's *Biographical Anecdotes* assert that her body was dissected by a Professor Martyn, who later donated her skeleton, in a glass case, to the Botanic Garden in Cambridge. Amongst the skeletal exhibits which were later moved from there to the Museum of Biological Anthropology, of the skeletons the Museum still holds, while several can be identified as female, none, with any certainty, can be identified as Sarah Malcolm.

Perhaps had the prolific Hogarth still been alive (he died in 1764) he would have relished taking Mary's likeness, reinforcing a brand of celebrity foreshadowing the high minded Victorian morality that would affect and determine who was thought to be deserving of fame. In this context, criminals still held the limelight. It is tempting to put flesh on the remaining bones of Mary Bateman and visually and metaphorically bring to life a woman who has been dead for over two centuries, but this is almost impossible given the sources. Only one near contemporary image of Mary is available to us, that being the engraving for the frontispiece of *The Extraordinary Life*, where she is shown holding up in her right hand the spurious hen's egg bearing the inscription 'Crist is coming'. In his *Lives of Twelve Bad Women* published in 1897, Arthur Vincent, who featured Mary alongside other notable villainesses who were 'consistently bad' such as the infamous

Moll Cutpurse and the aristocratic poisoner Frances Howard, the Countess of Somerset, stated that:

> 'There is no worthy likeness of the 'Yorkshire Witch', nothing but a rough cut prefixed to the "Extraordinary Life and Character of Mary Bateman", which is here reproduced in all its native barrenness.'

Whether the artist engraver had actually seen Mary in life we cannot know. Her face is certainly bereft of any expression or emotion, no more revealing than the plaster cast death mask taken from her skull which until recently was still on display in the Thackray Medical Museum alongside her partial skeleton, or that of the 3D render of Mary's face undertaken by University College London in 2001, at the behest of a BBC television series. With regards to the engraver responsible for Mary's image, we can guess his identity thanks to a contributor to the 1868 volume of *Notes and Queries*, a long-running quarterly scholarly journal founded in 1849 as an academic correspondence magazine, in which scholars and interested amateurs could exchange knowledge on folklore, literature and history. A certain Mr Edward Riggal of Bayswater, in possession of one of the 'ten thousand copies' of *The Extraordinary Life*, a second edition of the book, noted the 'curious portrait – inscribed "Mary Bateman, the Yorkshire Witch. Topham, sc. Leeds".' However, the engraver's name is not visible on the frontispiece engravings featured in the reproduction copies of *The Extraordinary Life* available as a reprint today. While the name of Topham is usually associated with the Leeds-born watercolourist and engraver Francis William Topham, as he was born in 1808, the year prior to Mary's execution, it would seem likely that the Mary Bateman engraving was executed by Francis's uncle Samuel Topham, born in Kirkgate in Leeds in 1788, and to whom the young Francis was apprenticed as an engraver. The 'sc.' added to the Topham name indicates the Latin 'sculpsit'; many early bank note engravers using 'sc' as the equivalent of saying 'Engraved by…'. As to the authorship of *The Extraordinary Life*, attributed to 'Anonymous', another entry in the 1868 *Notes and Queries* leads to the suggestion that the book may well have been written by Edward Baines who was also responsible for the book's publication, printed by Davis & Co based in Vicar Lane in Leeds. As well as being a politician, an MP for Leeds in the 1830s, Baines was a newspaper proprietor (he bought the *Leeds Mercury* in 1801) and the author of numerous historical and geographic works of reference. Amongst his best-known writings are *The History, Directory and Gazetteer of the County of York* and a *History of the Wars of Napoleon*; it is not beyond the realms of possibility that he was responsible for writing *The Extraordinary Life,* a work of 'moral reflections' as he must have been acutely aware of Mary's newsworthy trial and execution.

Returning to the engraving, Mary was described as having 'nothing ingenuous in her countenance, it had an air of placidity and composure'. Perhaps if the artist were Samuel Topham, and he had not actually laid eyes on his subject in life, then he was borrowing from this description. Mary was also described as 'neat in her person and dress'; certainly this is how she is presented in the illustration. Her clothes are befitting of a housewife of her time and station in life: the de rigueur neckerchief and mob cap, along with the clean white apron worn over the high-waisted 'Empire line' gown representative of the most popular and fashionable style of dress in the early nineteenth century. It is likely that Mary would actually have worn a dress made from a harder wearing material such as a light wool of brushed cotton as opposed to the more expensive and less functional muslin and silks worn by her social superiors.

Visual images, or lack of them, aside we are reliant for details of Mary's life on the heavily moralising *The Extraordinary Life*, which must be considered as something of a sensationalised and indeed unsubstantiated account, whoever wrote it. From a near contemporary point of view, other than the chapter given over to Mary in the second volume of *The Criminal recorder: or, Biographical sketches of Notorious Public Characters*, written in 1815, itself borrowing heavily from *The Extraordinary Life*, and the colourful though brief account of her life and crimes as reported by *The Newgate Calendar*, there is little else to draw on. The *Calendar* was a hugely popular monthly bulletin, yet a supposedly moralising publication that gave vivid accounts of notorious criminals in the eighteenth and nineteenth centuries. It was remarked that if an individual owned two books, one was the Bible and the other the *Newgate Calendar*, which did not disappoint in the report of Mary's case, opening with the line:

> 'The insidious arts practised by this woman rendered her a pest to the neighbourhood in which she resided, and she richly deserved that fate which eventually befell her.'

Though numerous brief accounts of Mary Bateman proliferate, they were written to warn against and perpetuate the stereotype of the 'dangerous' woman, to be heeded by other potential malefactors. Exhuming the real woman from the lurid accounts of her life is difficult to say the least, and that is why this book does not pretend to be a 'biography' in any conventional sense. Of necessity the preceding chapters rely to a certain extent on conjecture, yet in the instances where 'hard' evidence is lacking, there is too much 'soft' evidence to be brushed aside entirely.

Whereas today the high profile of the exploits of any insidious criminal is aired in any number of media formats, giving a clear image and insight into that person's life and motivation, the principal conundrum for the modern historian is sifting the historical record of the often biased past presented in line with history's censoring hand. Though Mary Bateman was and still is regarded as possessing a perfidious personality, resorting to psychoanalysis and intuition to fill in the blanks of her life and character, in the absence her own words, and any concrete and less biased biographical detail, is risky. Aside from the affecting letter she wrote to her husband from the condemned cell the night before her execution, the only other correspondence recorded are those conning letters written in the alleged hand of Miss Blythe. Even so, it is the duty of the historian to offer as full an explanation as possible for the events of the past and we have to try with Mary.

She began her career with thefts and frauds. Were these acts the results of feelings of anger, loss, disempowerment or social inadequacy rather than sheer economic need or greed as is so often the case with many compelled to steal? The factors supposedly influencing those who are today 'addicted' to shoplifting, include increasing stress, materialism, emptiness, and addiction in our society and world as a whole. Were such factors operating in Mary's day? The stress of survival in the harsh materialism of the new industrial cities must have been immense. She tended to defraud those of her own class, which meant that they trusted her. Colloquially known as a 'long game', a confidence trickster attempts to defraud a person or group after first gaining their confidence in exploiting characteristics of the human psyche. In Mary's case she played on her victims' inherent fears. Yet in view of the extremity of her later misdeeds, consideration must be given as to whether Mary Bateman was suffering from a psychological disorder, and should be branded either a psychopath or a sociopath, the professional terms for what psychiatry calls an antisocial personality disorder.

Broadly speaking, with regards to such complex psychological conditions, both types of personality disorder could have been applicable to Mary. Both have a pervasive pattern of disregard for the safety and rights of others, with deceit and manipulation central features to either type of personality. Contrary to popular belief, a psychopath or sociopath is not necessarily violent, as was the case with Mary Bateman, who relied on her own cunning to achieve her ends. The shared common features of diagnosed psychopaths and sociopaths include regularly flouting or breaking the law and perhaps most markedly feeling no remorse in their actions. In examining the traits of both of these complex, multifaceted conditions, the question of nature versus nurture is brought to the fore. While the clues to psychopathy and sociopathy are usually available in childhood, where a pattern of behaviour indicative of the violation of the basic rights or safety of others, and breaking rules and societal norms manifest at a young age, researchers generally believe that at variance to sociopaths, psychopaths tends to be born, and not 'made' and that they are subject to a genetic predisposition. Mary was, after an incidence of petty theft, marked out as being of a 'knavish and vicious disposition' from the age of five. Possibly related to physiological brain differences, research has further shown that confirmed psychopaths have underdeveloped components of the brain commonly thought to be responsible for emotion regulation and impulse control. Difficulty in forming real emotional attachments with others consequently results in artificial, shallow relationships designed to be manipulated in a way that most benefits the psychopath, who rarely feels guilt regarding any of their behaviours, no matter how detrimental they might be to others. Yet psychopaths are often viewed as being charming and trustworthy, holding down a steady, normal day-to-day life, even having families and seemingly-loving relationships with a partner. *The Extraordinary Life* described Mary Bateman as possessing:

> 'an air of placidity and composure, not ill adapted to make a favourable impression on those who visited her. Her manner of

> address was soft and insinuating, with the affectation of sanctity. In her domestic arrangements she was regular, and was mistress of such qualifications in housewifery as, with an honest heart, would have enabled her to fill her station with respectability and usefulness.'

As a rule, when a psychopath engages in criminal behaviour, they tend to do so in a way that minimizes risk to themselves, having carefully planned their criminal activity to ensure they evade detection, with contingency plans in place for every possibility. Until the unravelling of the Perigo 'sting', this fits Mary Bateman like a glove. One also has to wonder, did Mary keep a mental note of the tally of those she had murdered? Perhaps, when in her last letter to her husband written from the condemned cell she maintained her innocence in respect of the murder of Rebecca Perigo (though she did acknowledge culpability to serial frauds) she was in denial, or simply merely detached from her feelings as a consequence of her psychological condition? It is highly likely that the Kitchin sisters and their mother were also Mary's victims, which accounts for her place in criminal history as what the Victorians called a 'multiple murderer'.

In turn, unlike their psychopathic counterparts, sociopaths are believed to be the product of 'nurture' (the result of environmental factors), a consequence of childhood trauma, physical or emotional abuse, the negative aspects of their upbringing. We have no means of establishing whether Mary's household was a loving one, though doubtless she would have been physically chastised for the theft of the Morocco shoes that marked out as being 'knavish' and 'vicious' at such a tender age, since corporal punishment was then the accepted norm. The early exposure in her formative years to the supposed detrimental influences of the unfavourably viewed gypsy population descending annually on her home town would doubtless have been viewed by her contemporaries as a contributory factor in her development of a psychological defect, had the science of psychology of course been in existence at the time. However, in general, sociopaths tend to be more impulsive and erratic in their behaviour, they may become agitated and angered easily and, in the eyes of others, sociopaths will appear to be very disturbed. Any crimes committed by a sociopath, including murder, will tend to be haphazard, disorganized and spontaneous rather than planned, and with little regard for the risks or consequences of their actions; the chances of being apprehended are increased, which tends to rule out this particular personality disorder being applicable to Mary. Her crimes were highly organized and co-ordinated.

While considering the possibility of an antisocial personality disorder being the driving force behind Mary's crimes, we should examine her methods. To use poison as a murder weapon takes planning and some degree of skill; a poisoner could never claim that the crime was committed in the 'heat of the moment' and this somehow makes the act seem controlled, premeditated and all the more sinister. Poison was popularly seen as a method of murder frequently employed by females; requiring no physical exertion, a crime committed by stealth and in private. *The Extraordinary Life* noted, and this was certainly pertinent to the murder of Rebecca Perigo, that 'death by poison may be as surely accomplished at a distance as on the spot', and in this respect perpetrators were also less likely to be found guilty if they were indeed caught. Since antiquity, women were the guardians of the domestic realm, and the keepers of the keys to the kitchen cabinets. The lady of the house was ideally placed to conveniently administer a poison as she was predominantly involved with the preparation of food and the management of and access to household remedies and 'medicines'. Though their pharmacological skills could be directed to the good – as Alfred Swaine Taylor, the eminent nineteenth century toxicologist is quoted as saying 'A poison in a small dose is a medicine, a medicine in a large dose is a poison' – knowledge of the poisons needed to induce abortions and eliminate inconvenient rivals nevertheless has done nothing to diminish the stereotype of the poisoning woman, a stock character throughout history.

Such a woman was epitomised from the earliest times by Cleopatra, who in the Roman imagination was a 'fatale monstrum' using poison not only to effect her own suicide but also on prisoners of war. She in turn influenced later portraits of *femmes fatales* like Lucrezia Borgia, (who, historians now believe, never killed anybody). The notion is bolstered by the fact that in Medieval times poison had become a popular method of despatch as the increase in the establishment of apothecary shops in many towns and cities offered the sale of substances for medicinal use that could also be employed for a more malign purposes. While by the time of Mary's conviction the development of analytical chemistry, albeit rudimentary, had already dawned, increasing the risk that a poisoner would be caught, poison was still seen as a popular method of murder. Indeed, in spite of the earliest convictions secured as a result of the presentation of forensic evidence in a court of law, that of Mary Blandy in 1752 as a consequence of Dr Addington's efforts, and the later indisputable test for the presence of arsenic developed by chemist James Marsh in 1836, it was still possible for the guilty to walk free because juries were loath to convict on forensic evidence alone. An artful defence lawyer could play on a jury's lack of scientific knowledge regarding chemical analysis, the confusion leading them to disregard it and return a verdict of not guilty

Murders and attempted murders aside, the year 1806 was probably more memorable for events of a greater national significance, such as Lord Nelson's state funeral, the death of Prime Minister William Pitt and Charles James Fox, then British foreign minister, introducing a bill to ban British ships from transporting slaves to foreign countries. This was also the year of Mary's most notable fraud, in view of the sheer number of people she duped – the 'miracle egg' episode. Not only injurious to the egos of those taken in (and of course the poor chicken she employed as the vehicle for her hoax) the consequences of her fraudulent and blatant profiteering were certainly detrimental to the reputation of Joanna Southcott.

Another aspect of Mary's case piquing the curiosity of her contemporaries, as well as those who have become acquainted with her story in the two hundred years and more since her execution, stems from the incredulity at her ability to systematically steal and defraud people when she was already well known to be a thief and a trickster. Why wasn't she informed on by the people of Leeds? The probable explanation is that they were more afraid of her supposed abilities as a witch than the consequences of her predations. It would be easy to brand William Perigo, amongst others, as entirely naive for allowing himself to be so completely taken in by Mary, but no doubt, as the medical profession could offer no orthodox treatment to remedy his wife's condition, he sought assistance elsewhere. It was his and his wife's misfortune that they happened to enlist the services of one of the most pernicious women of her age.

Certainly the allusion to witchcraft darkly tinged Mary's name. As evidenced by those amongst the crowd gathered to witness her execution, believing to the very end that 'The Yorkshire Witch' would save herself from death at the last moment by employing her supernatural powers to vanish into thin air as the noose tightened, her supposed craft was very real to her contemporaries; especially to Winifred Bond. Sometimes employed by Mary to run various errands for her, when Winifred's testimony at Mary's trial was questioned by Judge Le Blanc, she affirmed that she was 'obliged' to leave Leeds at Mary Bateman's insistence as 'she was afraid', fearing the supernatural powers which she supposed Mary to possess. It was after all Rebecca Perigo's belief in the supernatural causes of her ailment, particularly the allusion to the 'black dog', an age old phenomenon believed to be an omen of death, which opened the Perigos' door to Mary's malign ministrations in the first place.

Although the last witch to be executed in England, Alice Molland, went to the gallows in Exeter in 1684, it was not until 1727 that the last witch in Scotland was burned at the stake. A Witchcraft Act was passed in 1735 which made it a crime for anyone to claim that a person had magical powers. Even so, witchcraft remained as a felony on the statute book until 1951. At Mary Bateman's trial, many who genuinely feared her alleged powers gathered outside the courtroom, giving all the more credence to those who had fallen victim to her reputation. It is easy to feel distanced today from the accounts of Mary's supposed witchcraft; people believed in things that we would no longer consider threatening, and indeed they acted in ways we might consider barbaric. We have become less credulous of 'magic' and more rigorous in our demand for empirical evidence, and in our modern technological age we pride ourselves on our rationality and scientific understanding of the world. Yet the vestiges and the power of the belief in evil remain. Believe it or not, the Church of England continues to perform exorcisms, though church representatives assert that most cases have conventional explanations, and actual exorcisms are quite rare. Nonetheless the 'Deliverance ministry' set up in 1974 makes provision for every diocese in the country to be equipped with a team trained in exorcism. Many still consider the 'evil' inherent in the actions of child killers, drug dealers, paedophiles, those responsible for genocide, ethnic purges, humanitarian atrocities and terrorists to be examples of the work of the devil. Now as in the past we are afraid, and at times of crisis fear still leads and fuels our beliefs and actions. In the current climate post 9/11 and the 'War on Terror' it could be said that we can still build policy on paranoia, to react, some would even say over-react, to certain situations in the name of security and feel threatened by an unseen enemy, finding ourselves behaving in ways frighteningly similar to those with an unshakeable conviction in the supposed powers exercised by Mary Bateman in the late 18th century, and certainly uppermost in the minds of those populating the public galley, and those who thronged outside the courtroom when her case came to trial.

In 2001, Daru Rooke, social historian and the curator of Cliffe Castle in Keighley, made a series for BBC2 entitled 'People Detectives' in which he took 'ordinary' people and led them stage by stage through the process of discovering their extraordinary ancestors. The first episode of the series, where Mary Bateman's five-times great granddaughter was introduced to the partial remains of her infamous forebear – at the time housed in a custom made box in the Thackray Medical Museum's archives – was needless to say of particular interest. The focus of the programme was heavily directed toward Mary being popularly regarded as a witch. In the opening minutes, Rooke's own superstitious proclivities were made apparent, with his particular reliance on a 'witch ball', a hollow sphere of reflective coloured glass suspended from his study ceiling intended to ward off evil spirits. He described Mary as a 'rum lot', highlighting the advantage she took of the literal belief in witchcraft prevalent at the time, though in his commentary, he was careful to note that Mary was in fact never tried as a witch. In addition to the 'bizarre family reunion' orchestrated in the Thackray's archives, the relatively new, at the time, resource of 3D modelling was applied to Mary Bateman's skull at University College London. The resultant lack of familial likeness to Mary's descendant was less than surprising however, considering that only 1.5 per cent of Mary's DNA would have been passed down to her present day descendants. Interestingly enough, Mr Rooke estimated the size of the crowd at Mary's execution to be 20,000. Other sources stipulate the more conservative figure in the region of 5,000, though Knipe's *Criminal Chronology*, 'carefully compiled' in 1867 'from prison documents, ancient papers, and other authentic sources', made note that for Mary's execution, 'The number of persons assembled was much greater than usual on such occasions'.

Obviously Mary Bateman's status as a 'witch' sensationalised her death, and as well as the monetary gains to be made from the sale of the broadsheet hawked at her execution, the barbaric treatment of her corpse post-mortem also presented a lucrative financial opportunity to commercially exploit her name. Yet, echoing the sympathies which rippled through the crowd on the day of her execution, feelings ran high with regard to the continual display for more than fifteen years of her skeletal remains, considered by some as wholly ill-fitting with the ethos of a progressive and scientific educational establishment such as the Thackray Medical Museum. Housed in one of the most impressive Victorian buildings in Leeds, formerly the 1861 Union Workhouse, the Thackray Medical Museum is truly unique and is the only museum of its kind in the North of England. Dedicated to preserving and bringing the past to life, exploring scientific breakthroughs and investigating surgical progress, the Museum's collection developed over the years enabling the wider public to learn more about the story of medicine. Opinions were nevertheless expressed that the display of an incomplete skeleton was of little educational benefit, beyond morbid shock value, and that to continue to display the remains of a woman executed over 200 years ago was disrespectful and excessive, Mary Bateman having paid the ultimate penalty for her misdeeds. Described by the Museum as one of their iconic exhibits long gripping the imagination of visitors to the Thackray, Mary's skeleton continued to attract great interest until the removal of the exhibit in summer 2015. It also caused controversy as to whether or not, over two centuries since her death, her remains should be given Christian burial, with the suggestion that the costs be borne by whoever has profited the most from the display of her bones.

While it may seem remiss not to include in a book about her life, and death, an image of Mary Bateman's skeleton, which was on public display for so many years, the omission is a deliberate one on my part. This is out of personal deference and respect, and in line with the Thackray Medical Museum's policy regarding photography of her remains continually in place up until the time the exhibit was finally removed. Affixed to the display case containing Mary Bateman's partial skeleton was a notice stating 'We respectfully request that visitors do not photograph or film the remains of Mary Bateman. This is in accordance with the Thackray Museum's policy on human rights. Please ask to speak to one of our curators if you require more information.'

This of course I did, and the Museum's Curator was kind enough to elaborate on the Thackray's policy, though they could not comment on the ultimate destiny of the remains at that time, as the exhibit was not actually the property of the Museum. In fact, the Thackray Medical Museum does not hold any human remains within their own collections, and instead 'loans in' human remains for appropriate displays from authorised sources, such as museums and science centres with correct tissue licenses and in line with ethical codes of practice. The remains of Mary still belong to Leeds University, and are legally part of the University's Anatomy Department, and have been since her body was first given over for dissection – hence the Thackray's policy on photography of this particular exhibit, as well as in deference to the human rights issue. In addition, the Thackray decided that it would be inappropriate to permit visitors to take photographs of Mary's remains in the museum, where they then may appear out of context with misappropriated information and have the potential to cause distress. Despite the Thackray's strictures on public photography, images of Mary's skeleton nevertheless proliferate on the internet and will doubtless continue to do so.

While the Mary Bateman exhibit proved a fascinating aspect of the Museum's displays, and enduringly popular with visitors, the final chapter of Mary Bateman's life is still waiting to be written. At the time of publication, her skeleton is now housed in Leeds University's Anatomy and Pathology Museum, which is in a private and secure room in the Medical School. The skeleton still forms part of the University's teaching collection, as it demonstrates an interesting anatomical variation that is still regarded as clinically relevant. It would appear that Mary Bateman had a 'cervical rib', an occasional congenital abnormality located above the normal first rib where a supernumerary rib can develop from the seventh cervical vertebra, sometimes known as a 'neck rib'. When the exhibit was removed at the end of June 2015 there was no publicity as the Thackray regarded the removal as a simple change of content in the gallery. While Leeds University had the final decision on removal, the Thackray agreed that as the display had been up for over fifteen years and ideally the museum look to change/rotate physically sensitive material periodically for conservation reasons, the continued display of Mary's skeleton was not considered a viable option for the future. Notwithstanding the incompatibility with current best practice for the redisplay of human remains in museums, the Thackray had also received a complaint from an individual stating he was a relative of Mary Bateman, and unhappy with the way her remains had been displayed.

The Thackray Museum and Leeds University have been in discussion about potentially showing a 3D printed version of the skeleton with additional interpretation around Mary's remains, with a view to also undertaking more research on her remains. However, this is subject to a funding bid. The space once occupied by the Mary Bateman exhibit currently holds a display of instruments used for medical dissections in the 1800s.

While there is no intention at present to bury or cremate the remains of Mary Bateman, in accordance with the University's policies and ethical procedures, the position will be reviewed on a regular basis. In 2004 the skeleton of William Corder, infamous for the murder of Maria Marten in the Red Barn in 1827, was released from the Hunterian Museum in London following lobbying from a descendant. After a religious service, the skeleton was cremated and buried in Corder's home village of Polstead, Suffolk. His scalp and a book bound in his skin remain on display at the Moyse's Hall Museum in Bury St Edmunds however.

Regardless of whether the legacy of damnation, as echoed in the heading of this chapter – a proclamatory line taken from *The Extraordinary Life,* still clings to the memory of The Yorkshire Witch, the question of a neglect in modern morality will doubtless continue to be a contentious issue. Human remains, particularly of those who gained a measure of notoriety in life, acquire new meanings as they pass through the hands of different practitioners, custodians, and collectors; consideration should be given to the journey such remains have taken to reach anatomy departments, museum displays, even the auction room, and whether or not Mary Bateman has indeed earned herself a measure of immortality, albeit by virtue of a dubious reputation, whether she is destined to 'rest in peace' – or in pieces – regardless of her name being damned 'to everlasting fame', only time will tell.

Bibliography and Sources

ANDREWS, DA & BONTA, James, *The Psychology of Criminal Conduct* Taylor & Francis Inc, Cincinnati, United States, 2010.

Anonymous, attributed to 'A.F.' Student of the Inner Temple, *The Criminal Recorder: or, Biographical sketches of Notorious Public Characters* J Cundee, London, 1815, Volume I.

BAILEY, Brian, *Hangmen of England,* WH Allen, London 1989.

BAINES, Edward (attrib), *The Extraordinary Life and Character of Mary Bateman, the Yorkshire Witch; Traced from the Earliest thefts of Her Infancy, Through a Awful Course of Crimes and Murders, Till Her Execution at the New Drop, Near the Castle of York, on Monday the Twentieth Of March, 1809.* Davis & Co, Vicar Lane, Leeds, 1811.

BARING-GOULD, Rev S, *Yorkshire oddities, incidents and strange events* John Hodges, London, 1874, Volume II.

BARTON-COHEN, Simon, *The Science of Evil: On Empathy and the Origins of Cruelty* The Perseus Book Group, Washington, United States, 2012.

BORROW, George Henry, *Celebrated Trials and Remarkable Cases of Criminal Jurisprudence from the Earliest Records to the Year 1825* Knight & Lacey, London,1825, Volume VI.

CHAPMAN, Pauline, *Madame Tussaud's Chamber of Horrors,* Grafton, London 1986.

COLE, Hubert, *Things for the Surgeon,* Heinemann, London, 1964.

CRITCHLEY, TA, *A History of Police in England and Wales,* Constable, London, 1967.

DAVIES, Owen, *Popular Magic: Cunning-folk in English History* Hambledon Continuum, London, 2007.

EMSLEY, Clive, *Crime and Society in England, 1750–1900.* Longman, Harlow 1987.

JAMES, PD and CRITCHLEY, TA, *The Maul and the Pear Tree,* Sphere, London 1987.

KNIPE, William, *Criminal Chronology of York Castle: With a Register of Criminals Capitally Convicted and Executed at the County Assizes, Commencing March 1st, 1379, to the Present Time* C. L. Burdekin, York, 1867.

NICHOLS, J, *Biographical Anecdotes of William Hogarth* London, 1785, 3rd edition.

PELHAM, Camden, *The chronicles of crime, or The new Newgate calendar. Being a series of memoirs and anecdotes of notorious characters who have outraged the laws of Great Britain from the earliest period to the present time including a number of curious cases never before published.*

RIVERS, Clarence T, *Personality Disorders and Mental Illnesses : The Truth about Psychopaths, Sociopaths, and Narcissists* Createspace, United States, 2014.

ROSENTHAL, Laura J, *Nightwalkers: Prostitute Narratives from the Eighteenth Century* Broadview Press, 2008.

SHARPE, James, *Witchcraft in Early Modern England* Pearson, Harlow, 2001.

T Tegg, London, 1841, Volume 1.

VINCENT, Arthur, *Lives of twelve bad women: illustrations and reviews of feminine turpitude, set forth by impartial hands* T.F. Unwin, London, 1897.

WATSON, Mary Decima, *Topcliffe: A History* 1970.

WILSON, Ben, *Decency and Disorder*, Faber and Faber, London, 2007.

WORTLEY, Richard, *Psychological Criminology : An Integrative Approach* Taylor & Francis Ltd, Cullompton, 2011.

Morbid Curiosities: Medical Museums in Nineteenth-Century Britain.
Samuel J.M.M. Alberti, Oxford Scholarship Online, May 2011.

Exhibition Ethics - An Overview of Major Issues.
Andromache Gazi, Journal of Conservation and Museum Studies.

Notes & Queries, London, July–December 1868, Fourth Series, Volume II.

Execution Broadsheets Archive, 1806–1833, York Museums Trust, York Castle Museum.

Calendars of felons and gaol delivery for trials at the Assizes, 1785–1851; York Castle Gaoler's journals, 1824–1863, Explore York Libraries & Archives.

Records of the West Riding Court of Quarter Sessions, West Yorkshire Archive Service, Wakefield.

'Leodis' online archive, Leeds Library Information Service.

Leeds Mercury, The British Newspaper Archive.

Leeds Directory, 1798, University of Leicester's Historical Directories Collection.

Topcliffe Parish Records 1570–1957, North Yorkshire County Records Office, Northallerton.

Murder Act (1752), London: HMSO. (25 Geo 2 11, c 37).

MeasuringWorth.com, Purchasing Power of British Pounds from 1270 to Present.

FamilySearch.org, Historical Records Search.

Index

1861 Union Workhouse, 133

abortifacients, herbal, 26–7, 41
abortion, 11, 26, 31, 129
  herbs used for, 26
abortionist, xii, 26, 31, 51, 56
Addington, Dr, 63, 129
Age of Reason, 12
All Saints' Northallerton, 2
Anatomy Museum of Edinburgh Medical School, 118
Anchor Inn (Kirkgate), 44
Anne (queen), 18, 105
anti-monarchists, 19
antisocial personality disorder, 125–31
Apocalypse, 46–7
Appleby Horse Fair, 3–4
Archbishopric of York, the, 8
Arkwright, Richard, 61
Arsenic, 92
  forensic tests for, 35, 40, 62–4, 84, 97, 129
  poisoning by, xii, 35, 38, 62–3, 96
  sources of, 39–40, 95
  symptoms of, 36
  uses of, 97
Arsenic Act, 37
Asenby, 1–5, 7, 14–15
Assize Courts, 86
Atkins, Robert, 19
Atkinson, Mr, 62

Babylon the Great, fall of, 45
back-to-back houses, 13, 39, 42, 64
Bag's Alley (Skipton), 13
Baines, Edward, 20, 123
  The History, Directory and Gazetteer of the County of York, 123
  History of the Wars of Napoleon, 123
Balm of Gilead, 48–9
Bank, 42, 51
Banks, Peter, 56
Bar Croft, 64
Bar of the Inner Temple, 90
Barghests, 68
Bastilles, 52
Bateman, George, 21
Bateman, Jack, 95
Bateman, James, 21, 107–8
Bateman, John, 15, 17–19, 60, 91–2
  awareness of Mary's deeds, 23, 42
  children of, 20–1
  involvement of, 87–8
  the militia and, 23–4
Bateman, John (father-in-law), 19–20
Bateman, John (son), 20–1
Bateman, Maria, 21
Bateman, Mary
  as an abortionist, xii, 11, 13, 26, 31, 51, 56
  analysis of, 125–31
  antisocial personality disorder and, 125–31
  arrest of, 84–5
  birth of, 1
  broadsheets for, 118–19
  brother of, 59–61
  burial of, xii
  childhood of, 2–5
  children of, 20–1
  crimes and misdeeds, ix–xi, 9, 49–51
  death of, ix
  display of skeleton of, 133–5
  dissection of body of, 101, 115
  as a domestic servant, 6–7
  employment history of, 8–9
  engravings of, 121–3
  fraud in prison, 110
  hanging of, 112–15, 132–3
  and John Bateman (father-in-law), 19

letter to husband, 109, 125
letters of, 19–20, 109
marriage of, 15, 21
as a military wife, 24–5
miraculous egg of, 46–8, 130
as a mother, 20
murders and, 32, 86, 90
and the Perigos, 68–81
pregnancy announcement of, 103
sentencing of, 99–101
siblings of, 2
sister-in-law of, 60–1
skeleton of, 117–18
skin of, 116
skull of, 3D modelling of, 132
and the Snowdens, 64, 67–8
tongue of, 117
trial of, 63, 90–1
defense of, 97–9
expert witnesses and, 95–6
the jury in, 99
possible defense and, 96–8
viewing of body of, 115
as a witch, 11, 15
Bateman, Mary (daughter), 21
Batemans, the, moving house and, 42, 62, 64
Bayswater, 122
BBC2, 132
belly, pleading the, 104–5
Berlin Criminal Police, x
Biographical Anecdotes (Hogarth), 121
Biographical sketches of Notorious Public Characters, 124
bitter buttons, 27
Black Dog Inn/pub, 42, 69
Black Dog Yard, 42, 44, 48, 69, 70, 71
black witch, 55
Blackstone, William (judge), 90
Commentaries, 90
Blake Street, 112
Blandy, Francis, 63
Blandy, Mary, 63–4, 129
blind back houses, 13
Blue Boar Inn, 102
Blythe, Miss, x, 32, 34, 54–9, 64–5, 67
letters of, 91, 97–8
and the Perigos, 69–79, 80–4, 88
Boar Lane, 19
Boardingham, Elizabeth, 89
Bolling Hall Museum, 117
Bond, Winifred, 58–9, 93–4, 97–8, 130
Book of Revelation, 45–6
Boot & Shoe Yard (Kirkgate), 43
Borgia, Lucrezia, 129
Borough Corporation Act, 84
Botanic Garden (Cambridge), 121
Botany Bay, 113
bough houses, 4
Bowling, 65
Boyle, Lord Justice-Clerk, 118
Bradford, 13–14, 65, 67, 82, 87, 117
Bradford Humbug Poisoning, 35
Bramley, 67–71, 76, 80, 82, 90, 93
Bravo, Charles, 98
Bridge Gate, 18
Briggate, 17–19, 53
bringer, the, 28
broadsheets, 108, 118–19, 133
Brompton, 2
Brompton by Northallerton, 1
Brothers, Richard, 44–6
Brown, Joseph, 113, 115
broadsheets for, 118–19
Brown, Reverend George, 108, 110, 114
Bubonic plague, 39
Burgan, Mary, 105
Burke, William, 116, 118
Buxton, 81–2, 93

cadavers, need for, 101
Cahill, Elizabeth, 106
Calendar of Felons for York Castle, 105
Call Lane (Leeds), 20, 95
Camp Field, 64
Camp Hill Court, 40
care-dependent children, 21, 107
Carpenter, James, 10
Carr, John, 86
Castle Mills Bridge, 112
Catholic Church, 101
cellar-dwelling Irish, 61
Chadwick, Edwin, 42
Chamber of Horrors, 116
Chapman, Pauline, *Madame Tussaud's Chamber of Horrors*, 116
Charity Children, 52
Charles II (king), 19, 85
Charlies, 85
charms, xii, 4, 25, 30–1, 55–6, 65, 72, 85, 116

Chief Constable of Leeds, 67, 84–5, 95
children
  born in prison, 105–7
  care-dependent, 21, 107
  employment of, 10, 12
  illegitimate, 19
cholera epidemics, in Leeds, 43
cholera morbus, 35
Chorley, Thomas, 80–1, 95–6, 98, 116–17
Church of England, 131
City Square, 23
Cleopatra, 129
Clerk of the Arraigns, 103
Cliffe Castle (Keighley), 132
cloth market, 18
Clough, Mr, 95
coaching inns, 8
Commentaries (Blackstone), 90
Commercial Street, 18
Constables of the Watch, 48, 85
Constabulary Act, 84
Coopers, the, 31–2
Corder, William, 116, 136
cotton mills, 61
Cottonopolis, 61
Countess of Somerset, 122
County Arcade, 53
County Court, 86–7
Crimean War, 12
Criminal Chronology (Knipe), 132
Criminal recorder, The, 124
Croft-on-Tees, 33, 81
Crookes, Mr, 44
Cross Green Lane, 42
Cryer, Judith, 57–9
Crystal Palace, 12
Cumbria, 3
cunning folk, 34, 55–6
Curry, William 'Mutton,' 113–14
Curzley, Dr, 68
Cutpurse, Moll, 122

Davis & Co, 123
dead bodies, protection of, 102
death, portents of, 47, 68, 131
Debtor's Prison, 86
DeFoe, Daniel, *Moll Flanders*, 104
Deliverance ministry, the, 131
dissection, 38, 40, 52, 101–2, 116, 134–5
Dixon, Mr, 16
Dobbin, Thomas, 75, 93, 97
domestic servant, 5–6, 26
Doomsday prediction, xi, 47
Duffield, William, 84–5, 95
Duncomb, Lydia, 121
Dunning, Ann, 1

East Street, 42
Eboracum of the Romans, 8
Edward III (king), 3
egg, *see* miracle egg
'Egyptians,' the, 3
Elmhirst, Robert, 117
Elmhirst, William, 116
End Days, xi
England
  French invasion of, 24
  living conditions in, 12–13
English common law, 104
English Reformation, 101
Errington, John, 19
Examen of Witches, 56
execution, public, 89, 111, 118
exorcisms, 131
Express, the, 8
The Extraordinary Life and Character of Mary Bateman., xi, xiii, 16, 84,
  author of, 123
  description of Mary, 126–7
  her remains, debate about, 136
  image of Mary, 121–2
  final line of, 34
  magistrate at trial, 85
  murder by poison and, 128

factories, conditions in, 10
Farnley Wood plotters, 19
Farr, William, 36
Farrow, Elizabeth, 34
fatale monstrum, 129
female criminality / criminals, 88, 105–6, 120–2
  society and, 88–9
femmes fatales, 129
Fenham Barracks, 60
Fenton, Mr, 83
Ferrybridge, 113
fight, stand up, 4
fire brigades, 22
Fisher, Rebecca, 51

Fishguard (Pembrokeshire), 24
Fletcher, Elizabeth, 113
Fletcher, Sarah, 113
folk healer, 55
followers, sealing of, 46–7
forensic evidence/test, 63–4, 129
Fox, Charles James, 129
Franco-Spanish fleet, 60
French and Napoleonic Wars, 24

Gallytorts, 68
General Infirmary, benefit of, 115
General Register Office, 36
Gennat, Ernst, x
George III (king), 2, 46
George IV (king), 117
Good Friday cake, 38
Gosling, Joseph, 62
Gosling family, 62–4
Great Fire of London, 12
Great Sessions, 86
Great Wilson Street, 40
Green, Hannah, 13–14
Greenwood, Mr, 27
Greenwood, Mrs, 27–8
Gristy, Thomas, 95, 98
gypsies, x, 3–4, 26

Haarmann, Fritz, x
Haddon, Peter, 21
Halfpenny, Joseph, 112
Hampsthwaite, 37
Hardy, John, 90–2
Harker, Ann (nee Dunning), 1, 61
Harker, Ann (sister), 2
Harker, Benjamin, 1
Harker, Benjamin (brother), 2
Harker, Elizabeth, 2
Harker, Jane, 2
Harker, John, 2
Harker, Mary, 1, 15. *See also* Bateman, Mary
Harkers (the), 2
Harper, Anne, 38
Harper, Thomas, 38
Harper, William, 38
Harrison, Elizabeth, 121
Harrogate, 33, 37, 81
Haworth, 94
Hebrews, Prince of, 44, 46
hen, miraculous egg of, 11, 46–8, 51, 121, 130
Hensal, 113
herbal abortifacients, 26–7, 41
Hereford, signs in the skies, 47
Hick, William, 93, 97
High Court Lane, 15, 17
Highflyer, the, 8
History, Directory & Gazetteer of Yorkshire, 119
History, Directory and Gazetteer of the County of York (Baines), 123
History of the Wars of Napoleon (Baines), 123
Hogarth, 120
  Biographical Anecdotes, 121
Holbeck, 22, 62
Hollings, Naomi, 106
Horseman, 37
Howard, Frances, 122
Howgate, Rose, 94, 98
human skin, preservation of, 116–17, 136
Huncoates (Lincolnshire), 47
Hunterian Museum (London), 136

Ilkley, 33, 81, 117
illegitimate children, 19
Industrial Revolution, 2, 9
infanticide, 26
inheritance powder, 36
Ireland, 24
Irish, cellar-dwelling, 61
iron coffins, 102

Jamie, Daft, 116
Jesus Christ, return of/the second coming of, xi, 44
Jews, 45
Jorvik, 8
judges, in the 17th and 18th centuries, 90
jury of matrons, 104–5, 107

Kilnsey Crag, 13
King Edward Street, 53
King's Bench, 90
Kirkgate Market, 18
Kirkstall Bridge, 70, 71
Kitchin, Mrs, 34–5
Kitchin deaths, 41, 108, 127
  autopsy request, 40
  investigation of, 38–9

Kitchin, Misses, xii, 33–5
Knaresborough's Prophetess, 12
Knavesmire gallows, 111–12
Knipe, *Criminal Chronology*, 132
Kurten, Peter, x

Lady Fair Day, 3
Lady Lane, 52
Lady Lane Workhouse, 52
Lawson, Dr, 96
Le Blanc, Mr Justice Simon, 87, 90, 93–4, 99, 107, 130
Leeds, 9
  Bubonic plague in, 39
  cholera epidemics in, 43
  parish workhouse in, 52
  population of, 9
Leeds Benevolent Society, 29
Leeds Bridge, 18, 53
Leeds Coach office, 93, 97
Leeds Directory, 20, 95
Leeds General Infirmary, 23, 115, 117
Leeds Intelligencer newspaper, 110
Leeds Market, 106
Leeds Medical School, 117
Leeds Mercury, 20, 67, 123
Leeds Minster, 21
Leeds Trade Directory, 18
Leeds University Anatomy Department, xii, 134
Leeds University's Anatomy and Pathology Museum, 135
Lent Assizes, 87
License Register, The, 49
Ling Bob Witch, 13–15
Lion & Lamb Inn, 75, 88
Lives of Twelve Bad Women (Vincent), 121
living conditions, of the working class, 42–3
Loudun, 55
Low Petergate, 119
Lucas, James, 96
Luddites, 114
Lumley, Peggy, 14–15

M. Bateman's Balm of Gilead, 48–9
Madame Tussaud's Chamber of Horrors (Chapman), 116
magic, 12, 56–7, 65, 71, 83, 131
Maiden's Bower maze, 5
Malcolm, Sarah, 120–1
Manchester, xi, 36, 61–2, 98
mantua maker, 11, 15
Marble Arch, 103
Market Cross, 3
Marlborough House, 117
Marsh, James, 129
Marsh Lane, 25, 44, 83
Marshall, Eliza, 43
Marshall & Benyon flax mill, 22, 64
Marshall & Co, 10
Marten, Maria, 116, 136
Martyn, Professor, 121
Masonic Lodge, 14
mass poisoning, 35–6
matrons, jury of, 104–5, 107
Maude, Miss, 23
May Day, 5
Maybrick, Florence, 39–40
Maybrick, James, 98
Meadow Lane, 53, 62
mentha pulegium, 26–7
Merrington, George, 112
Merrington, Maria, 112
Methley Hall, library of, 117
Micklegate Bar, 112
Middle East, 49
Middle Row, 19
militia, supplementary, 23–4
Mill Bank, 4
Millenarianism, 46
miracle egg, xi, 11, 46–8, 51, 121, 130
Miss Blythe, x, 32, 34, 54–9, 64–5, 67
  letters of, 91, 97, 98
  and the Perigos, 69–79, 80–4, 88
Mitchell, T Carter, *Thirsk Falcon*, 14
Moll Flanders (DeFoe), 104
Molland, Alice, 12, 131
Moon Men, the, 3
Moore, Mrs, x, 25–6, 27, 30
Moot Hall, 18–19
mortsafes, 102
Mother Shipton, 11–12
Moyse's Hall Museum, 136
Mr Fenton's 83
Mr Stubbs' Private Museum, 117
Mrs Moore, x, 25–6, 27, 30
Mrs Smith, 17
Murder Act, 101, 102
Murphy, Christian, 105
Museum of Biological Anthropology, 121

Musgrave, Mr, 75
mutton, stolen, 53

Nelson, Lord, funeral of, 129
New Drop. *see* York's New Drop
Newcastle, 8, 56, 60
Newgate Calendar, The, 124
Newgate Gaol, 120
Newton, Isaac, 54
Nightingale, Florence, 23
non-capital punishments, 104
North Riding of Yorkshire, 1
Notes and Queries, 116–17, 122–3

Old Assembly Rooms (Kirkgate), 51
Old Nan, 13–14
Order and Indictment Books for Leeds
  Quarter Sessions, 87
orthodox Christian beliefs, scamming and,
  44–9
Ouse, river, 112

Palmer, William, 98
pardons, granting of, 104–6
Park Road, 4
pawn shops, 11, 23
Peel, Robert, 16
penal code, reform of, 16
Pennyroyal (mentha pulegium), 26–7
  as abortion herbs, 26
People Detectives, 132
Perigo, Rebecca, xii, 66, 68–79, 85, 90, 109,
  127
  belief in the supernatural, 130–1
  poisoning of, 128
Perigo, William, 49, 68, 68–79, 97, 117, 130
  after wife's death, 80–4, 91
  diagnosis of poisoning and, 80
  and Mary Bateman's trial, 93–5
Perigos, the, poisoning of, 92
pickpockets, 3, 111
  penalties for, 16
Pitt, William, 129
poisoning, mass, 35–6
poisoning cases, 98, 128–9
post 9/11, 131
Potts, Hannah, 99
poudre de succession, 36
pregnancy, and stay of execution of, 104–5
Price, Ann, 121
Prince of the Hebrews, 44, 46
Prince of Wales, 117
prisoners, women, and care-dependent
  children, 21, 107
proclamations of faith, 47
Prophet Hen of Leeds, The, xi
prostitutes/prostitution, 3, 11
  as nurses, 23
psychic industry, the, 54
psychological gratification, and murder, x
psychopaths, 125–8
public execution, 89, 111, 118
public justice, 108
puddling grass, 27

Quarry Hill (Leeds), 33, 39, 81
Quarter and Petty Sessions, 87
Quarter Sessions, 86–87

Raikes, Robert, 6
Recorder for the Borough of Leeds, 90
recruiting sergeant, 28
Red Barn, 116, 136
Rede, *York Castle in the Nineteenth Century*,
  109
Resurrection Men, the, 101–2
Revolution (1789), 52
Rhodes, Joseph, 37
Rhodes, Thomas, 37
Riggal, Edward, 122
River Swale, 1
Rogerson, John, 94
Romany people, 4
Rooke, Daru, 132
Royal Mail, 8
Royal Navy, 59

Salem, 55
Sanitary Conditions in Leeds report, 43
Sayers, Dorothy L, 120
Scarborough, 34, 57, 70–3, 85, 92, 99
Scientific Revolution, the, 54
screw down/screwer-down agent, 25–8, 30
Shambles, The, 53
Shiloh of Genesis, 45
Shucks, 68
slaves, transportation of, 129
Smith, William, 38
Smith, Mrs, 17
Snowden, James, 64, 67, 87

Snowden, Mrs, 64–5
Society of Friends, 33–4
sociopaths, 125–8
Somerset, Countess, 122
South Coast, 24
Southcott, Joanna, xi, 44–5, 48, 130
Southcottians, 45–6, 49–50
Southill, Ursula, 11–12
spa resorts, 33–4, 81
spectral hounds, 68
St Columba, Topcliffe, 1
St George's Churchyard, 102
St Peter's Church (Leeds), 15, 21, 108
St Peter's Square (Leeds), 33
St Peter's Well, 33
St Thomas (parish church), 2
stand up fight, 4
Stanningley, 71
Stead, Barzillai, 27–8
Stead, Mrs, 28–9
Stead, Sarah, 68–9, 92–3, 97
Stead family, the duping of, 27–31
Stephenson, Miss, 16–17
Stockdale, Joshua, 94–5
Storry, William, 119
Stranger's Friend Society, 29
Sutton, Mr, 75, 88
Swale, River, 1
Sykes Lane, 4

tanacetum vulgare, 27
Tansy (tanacetum vulgare), as abortion
  herbs, 26–7
Taylor, Alfred Swaine, 128
tea leaves, reading of, 13–14
Thackray Medical Museum, xii, 118, 122,
  133–5
Thackray Medical Museum's archives, 132
The Three Tuns, 8
The Times, 113
theft, penalties for, 16
Thirsk, 1, 5, 7–8, 19, 20, 64, 113
Thirsk Falcon, 14
Three Legged Mare, 111
Three Ridings, 105, 107
Timble Bridge, 25
Tone, Wolfe, 24
Topcliffe, 1, 3, 5
Topham, 122–3
Topham, Francis William, 122
Topham, Samuel, 122–3
Topley Fair, 3, 5, 14
Topley Fair gypsies, 26
Town Cryer, 19
Trash marauds, 68
Travellers, 4
Trinity Hall (Cambridge), 90
turf labyrinths / mazes, 5
Turpin, Dick, 102, 112
Tussaud, Madame, 116
Lives of Twelve Bad Women (Vincent), 121
Twelve Tribes of Israel, 46
Tyburn Tree, 103, 111

Union Workhouse, 133
United Irishmen, 24
University College London, 122, 132
University of Edinburgh Medical School, 23

Vale of Mowbray, 5
Vicar Lane, 28, 52, 123
  Bubonic plague in, 39
Viking centre (Jorvik), 8
Vincent, Arthur, *Lives of Twelve Bad Women*,
  121

War on Terror, 131
Ward, Thomas, 105–6
watchtowers, 102
Water Lane, 22, 40, 64, 88, 92
Webster, Elizabeth, 106–7
Webster, William, 107
Wellesley, Arthur, 60
Wells, Mr, 17
Wells' Yard, 17–18, 25
Wesleyan Methodist church, 29
West Riding, Deputy Lieutenant for the,
  116
West Riding courts, 87
Wharfedale, 13
Whig government, 42
white witches, 55–6
Whitley, Hannah, 37–8
Whitsun 1806, 68
Wilford, Thomas, 102–3
Wilkes, John, 2
Williams, Mr, 90–1
Wilson, Harriet, 10
Wilson, Henry, 19
Winter, Nancy, 13–14

witch ball, 132
witch hunts, 12, 55
Witchcraft Act, 131
witches, 55–6
witches, in Yorkshire, 13
women prisoners, and care-dependent children, 21, 107
workhouses, 52
working classes, investigation into the, 42–3
Wright, Mr, 18–19, 91, 97

York, 8, 49
York Castle Gaol, 21, 86, 105–6, 111, 113
York Castle in the Nineteenth Century (Rede), 109
York Castle Museum, 112
York Herald, 111–12
York Museum Trust, 118
York Tyburn, 38, 89, 111
York's 'Female Prison, 86
York's Knavesmire gallows, 102
York's New Drop gallows, ix, xiii, 1, 111–12
Yorkshire Bank, 23
Yorkshire Constabulary, 48
Yorkshire Notes and Queries, 117
The Yorkshire Witch, the ix, 48, 114, 120, 130, 136. *See also* Bateman, Mary